A Call To Reform

Sustaining America's Unique Culture

Stephen P. Fish

A Call To Reform

Stephen P. Fish

First Edition 2020

ISBN 978-1-7345969-0-8

www. *ACallToReform* .com

Dedications

This publication is dedicated to my immediate family...my wife, Bruni, of forty-four years, and our children, Dave, Natalya, Stephanie, and Ben. We can always talk politics and government intelligently without the hatred and vitriol you hear in so many other places.

In addition, a special thank you goes out to my brother, John. His meticulous questioning of my rough ideas helped make the book something of value for anyone interested in understanding how the human rights and civil liberties Americans enjoy has created a unique American political, social, and economic culture.

Also, this publication is dedicated to the many wonderful students I taught and worked with in school and in clubs over the years. It is my sincere hope that (if not the current generation), their generation will adopt many of the ideas herein, fine-tune them and find a way to incorporate them into the government to build a better, more responsive America for all people, especially the middle class who works every day.

In addition, I would be remiss if I did not dedicate this publication to my friend of forty some years Ken Salazar, who time and time again, through discussions and phone calls and emails, encouraged me to rough out my ideas for reform. His tireless efforts in California, in editing and promoting the book, made this book a reality.

Also, to Guy D'Agostino, who gave me a real historical perspective of what it was like to live under a fascist regime during the 1930s, which did not allow its citizens the freedoms we have today. And thank you to Jill Fox who works with Guy. She gave me the inspiration to try and reach out to people, especially young people, to remind them how lucky they are to be living in America and enjoying so many human rights and civil liberties.

In addition, thank you so much to Kate, Cindy, and Eric for all our morning/lunch discussions about current events and reform ideas.

Also, thank you to my teacher mentor, Cathy, for all our discussions on not only secondary education but politics as well. She was and continues to be a great source of support. In addition, thank you to the many great teachers and administrators I worked with. Their professionalism inspired me to be as good a teacher as possible.

And, thank you to Tommy Salazar and Tracy Green. They helped me with specific ideas to improve the book by reading drafts and making suggestions.

Thank you so much to David D. Cree who not only designed the creative cover for this book, but was instrumental in getting it ready for publication. He was great to work with as well as his patience and creativity greatly appreciated.

Thank you also to the attorneys who helped with this project.

And finally, a special thank you goes out to Lowanna Owens, who was key in editing this book, and to the Librarians at the Pennsylvania State Library. Who without their help, as well as all the people mentioned above, the book may never have gotten beyond my laptop.

Throughout this book you will read about the following main themes...all important to achieving the goal of sustaining and fine-tuning our unique political, social and environmental American culture.

History

Governmental Reforms

Jobs

Healthcare

Education

Sustainability

Forward

As a former secondary education teacher, I generally told students, sometime during the year, I did not care what they looked like. I did not care what color or ethnicity they were. I did not care what religion they worshiped. I did not care if they were a citizen or an immigrant who recently came here with their family. I did not even care if they had a green card or could speak little English.

What I did care about was whether they knew what was in the *Declaration of Independence, The Constitution of the United States of America,* and the *Bill of Rights.* More importantly, did they believe in and support the time-tested Enlightenment ideas that are embedded in those documents? Of course, sometimes they answered me and other times they did not, which led me to wonder if they really knew what was in these incredible historical documents.

So, I would then approach it in a different way. I would ask them to tell me what it might be like to live in a country where people did not have the kinds of human rights and civil liberties we have, like for example, freedom of speech. The responses to this question were much better.

Later in the year, I sometimes would ask a friend of mine to visit our A.P. European History class to reinforce our previous discussions on civil liberties and freedom of speech. His description of events when he was young regarding freedom of speech always captivated the class and motivated a ton of questions. His real-life story went something like this:

When I was in elementary school in Italy, Benito Mussolini became the fascist dictator of Italy. Things changed rapidly under the fascist government of Mussolini during the 1930s. For example, one day someone from his street army, called "Black Shirts," visited my friends and I at elementary school. While there, the man took down a picture of Jesus Christ hanging in the church school and replaced it with a portrait of Benito Mussolini.

As I got older, I discovered that civil liberties people enjoyed were significantly curtailed under Mussolini's regime. Specifically, freedom of speech almost disappeared. For example, a few years later, when I was learning to be a barber, a government man came to the barber shop. It was a very busy day, but the government man ordered everyone to immediately leave the barber shop to attend a parade given in Mussolini's honor. When people protested, telling the man it was one of the busiest days of the week for haircuts, the man shouted and ordered them to leave immediately. They were also told they had to cheer at the parade as if they loved and adored Mussolini.

Then, on another occasion, a government man visited the barber shop again. But this time it was to speak with a gentleman about something he had said negative about the government. The government man was quite stern and serious about informing the man to stop saying anything negative about Mussolini or the government. If the gentleman getting his hair cut continued to make negative remarks in public, a second visit would be in order. Of course, chastising this man in public was done to set an example for others.

Unfortunately, the gentleman did not heed the warning. The government man returned. This time the gentleman was ordered to follow the government man. They went to a pharmacy and the government man bought ingredients to make a concoction. The government man, after making the concoction, forced the gentleman to drink it. The result was a bad case of diarrhea. Before the government man left, he warned the gentleman again about saying anything negative, either in public or to friends, about Mussolini and the government.

If it happened a third time, either one or two men would visit the man again. However, this time the man would be asked to go with the government men in a car. His family would never hear from him again.

Imagine living in a society like this. For Americans, having grown up in a country with free speech, it would be almost impossible to keep your opinions to yourself or not to voice objections at times, or not to protest government activity at times. Fortunately for Americans, we have safeguards to protect human rights and civil liberties. But, could anyone or could the government ever take away these precious human rights and civil liberties? How easy was it for Hitler in Germany to take away their human rights and civil liberties?

It was easier than one might think. The Nazis gained control of the government in 1932 and stripped people of their human and civil rights shortly thereafter by deception and dishonesty and the use of fascist tactics. It's a story of how they won enough seats in the Reichstag through a general election (democracy) to become the dominant party. It's a story of how they created an incident to strike fear in ordinary Germans, who then allowed the Nazis to change the course of history. Briefly, here is the story:

On the evening of Monday February 27, 1933, a fire was set in the Reichstag building (the German Parliament), which for all practical purposes resulted in destruction of the building. A recent immigrant to Germany, an alleged deranged communist unemployed bricklayer by the name of Marinus van der Lubbe, age 24, was blamed for the arson attack. He had been searching for a government building to burn down. It was his way of protesting capitalism. He decided on the Reichstag (The Reichstag Burns).

With the help of some Nazi storm troopers, led by SA leader Karl Ernst, (it is not sure he knew who they really were other than Ernst had befriended him in Berlin), they entered the cellar of the Reichstag through an underground tunnel connected to Nazi leader Goring's residence. Immediately they set about torching the building. Lubbe was eventually arrested and executed for the arson attack. Nothing happened to Ernst or the others because they had set Lubbe up to take the fall. They wanted to burn the Reichstag down, to scare the public into believing communists were about to stage a violent takeover of Germany. Historically, no proof of this has ever been discovered (The Reichstag Burns).

Nevertheless, Adolf Hitler used this incident to scare the cabinet into agreeing to what we would call marshal law today. He also went to the media of the day, newspapers, and gave a false story. In other words, he made up an emergency so that he could invoke a decree giving him more power. He also went to the old President of the Weimar Republic, Paul von Hindenburg and asked him to sign the "Reichstag Fire Decree." Thinking he was protecting Germany from a communist insurrection he signed the decree. That decree, among other things, revoked the civil liberties of people, including the right to free speech! It was for Hitler, the beginning of the total takeover of Germany by the Nazi party (The Reichstag Burns).

That's how easy it was. Hitler created a fake emergency by burning down the parliament, to take away people's civil liberties, including freedom of speech. These civil liberties, like freedom of speech did not return in Germany until 1945, when the allies liberated the German people after World War II.

The question today is what are the human rights and civil liberties Americans enjoy today and could they be taken away someday? To answer these questions, the first part of this book will discuss some of the more important human rights and civil liberties we have by examining a brief history of them. Then, we will examine where they are located in, "The Declaration of Independence," "The Constitution of the United States," and the "Bill of Rights and subsequent Amendments."

After that, we will discuss how we can fine-tune our government in the future to ensure we never lose our precious human rights and civil liberties as well as our unique American culture. It has been over 230 years since *The Constitution of the United States of America* was initially ratified to create the United States. And while some amendments and many laws have been added since then, it's still been a long time and many things have changed in the United States. For one, when the constitution was written and ratified, there were no political parties. Today the Democratic and Republican parties are so entrenched, and our politics so radicalized, it is difficult to get consensus on any important reforms. Part two of the book will address some important needed reforms. Also, the reform ideas mentioned herein are not meant to be an end in and of themselves. Rather, they are suggestions to jump start people talking about serious reform. They are starting points for people to begin a conversation about what they really think is best for America moving forward.

Then, in the last chapter, "**A Call To Reform**," we will discuss how you can become involved in a serious process to help fine-tune reform ideas. This process will include a website which we hope interested people from all fifty states and territories will soon visit.

Lastly, we hope you like the book and will learn more about what makes us uniquely American. We also hope the suggested reform ideas discussed herein can get people to begin seriously talking about important needed reforms! It's time. If this book can accomplish these things, then we will be able to make our governmental system better, minimize partisan politics and help sustain, for everyone and future generations, the human rights and civil liberties we all enjoy in our unique American political, economic, and social culture.

Table Of Contents

Historical Background

Did you ever wonder where the ideas and values came from that Thomas Jefferson wrote about and penned into *The Declaration of Independence*? Perhaps we need to step back a bit and look at the historical background of these ideas in order to better understand them.

Our story begins in the year 1215 A.D, during the reign of King John of England (1199-1216). Over the centuries, stories have arisen about what happened during King John's time. The legend of Robin Hood came from this time period. The book "Ivanhoe" also tells of that time period. In both stories, there is a theme of a corrupt king who believed he had the power to take people's possessions, impose whatever tax he wished upon his subjects or to imprison them or to pass judgement on them as he saw fit, including execution.

This seemingly abuse of power by King John raises the philosophical question of how to create a central government which is strong enough to suppress anarchy and protect its subjects from foreign invasion yet sets limits to an autocracy threatening to overshadow individual liberty. This question of how to obtain efficient government, often forces nations to choose between two types of rulers: One who restores order but tramples on his subjects, and one who isn't so strong but allows freedom for his subjects. England often struggled with this important question. In fact, the history of medieval England is the swinging of the pendulum back and forth between these two types of rulers. English history centers around the attempt to create a strong monarchy, and yet to set limits to its strength (McKechnie 4-6).

All of this came to a head on 15 June 1215 A.D. in a meadow called Runnymede, between Windsor and Stains. On that momentous day, the barons and the English Church forced King John to meet them and to sign a written document that emerged as one of the most important documents in human history. On that day, King John agreed to grant to all English freemen, certain liberties written in the document titled the, "Magna Carta," sometimes also called "The Great Charter of King John." Below are just a few articles from that document which years later, greatly influenced our founding fathers in America.

Article 1:   "We have granted to God, and by this charter confirmed for us and our heirs forever that the English church shall be free, and shall have the rights entire, and her liberties inviolate; We have also granted to all freemen of our kingdom, for us and our heirs forever, all the underwritten liberties, to be had and held by them and their heirs, of us and our heirs forever" (McKechnie 233).

In this article we see the groundwork laid for the concept of separation of church and state. Essentially, it says that neither church or freemen and their civil liberties were to be treated as of more importance than the other. Years later our founding fathers in the first amendment also spelled out that religious toleration was equally important as freedom of speech, freedom of the press and freedom to assemble.

Article 2:   "If any of our earls or barons, or others holding of us in chief by military service shall have dies, and at the time of his death his heir shall be of full age and owe relief, he shall have his inheritance on payment of the ancient relief..." (McKechnie 229).

Article 3:   "If, however, the heir of anyone of the aforesaid has been underage and in wardship, let him have his inheritance without relief and without fine when he comes of age" (McKechnie 239).

Chief among King John's abuses was his ability to arbitrarily increase feudal obligations. Articles 2 thru 5 give credibility to the complaints that King John and members of his government arbitrarily changed taxes/fines simply to gain more money, even when a person died. Today we have laws regarding inheritance taxes, and no one can raise an inheritance tax without a new law being passed and signed by the governor of a democratic legislature.

Article 7:   "A widow, after the death of her husband, shall forthwith and without difficulty have her marriage portion and inheritance..." (McKechnie 254).

Article 8:   "Let no widow be compelled to marry, so long as she prefers to live without a husband..." (McKechnie, 260).

Articles 6 thru 8 deal with women's rights. Article 6 addresses the king's right to regulate the marriage of wards. By the time of the *Magna Carta*, this had become an intolerable grievance.

Articles 7 and 8 noted above deal with the right of a woman to remarry as well as her right to inherit her property as well as her husband's. Years later, English philosopher John Locke wrote about the right of any person to own and inherit property. These concepts also made their way into American culture via the ratification of the fourteenth amendment. It reaffirmed the equality of women and their right to own property.

Article 12: "No scutage nor aid shall be imposed in our kingdom unless by common counsel of our kingdom…" (McKechnie 275).

This clause developed into the modern-day doctrine that the crown cannot impose any financial burden whatsoever on the people without the consent of Parliament. In America our founding fathers agreed with this concept. They did not want any arbitrary taxes or excessive financial burdens like stamp taxes without having representation in Parliament. The key word is "excessive." Today we still struggle with what are excessive taxes. Yet we all agree the President cannot arbitrarily impose any taxes upon Americans without the approval of Congress.

Article 13: "The citizens of London shall have all their ancient liberties and free customs, as well by land and by water, furthermore, we decree and grant that all other cities, boroughs, towns and ports shall have all their liberties and free customs" (McKechnie 284).

Most important in the list of liberties was the ability of London and other principalities to freely appoint a mayor and to choose their own sheriff (McKechnie 284). Today, this is a tenant of democracy everywhere.

Article 14: "For obtaining the common counsel of the kingdom anent the assessing of an aid or of a scutage we will cause to be summoned the archbishops, bishops, abbots, earls, and greater barons..." (Mckechnie 292).

Herein we see the general doctrine of representation. This article is evidence that the framers of the *Magna Carta* had grasped the principle that taxation and representation go together. Our founding fathers also had grasped this concept which is why they petitioned King George III over and over again about no taxes without representation.

Article 15: "We will not for the future grant to any one license to take an aid from his own free Tenants..." (McKechnie 302).

In this article, the barons were trying to protect ordinary people who were tenants. Their Lords were no longer arbitrarily able to extort money from them. This concept of laws for everyone, whether they were a member of the nobility or not, made its way into American documents with the prohibiting of anyone ever being given a title of nobility and wealthy people are subject to the same laws as anyone else.

Article 17: "Common pleas shall not follow our court, but shall be held in some fixed place" (McKechnie 308).

It was very expensive to try and defend yourself in court because the court traveled with the king. So, this article was an attempt to make royal justice cheaper and more accessible by holding the court in one fixed, pre-appointed place.

Article 24:   "No sheriff, constable, coroners, or others of our bailiffs shall hold pleas of our Crown" (McKechnie 358-359).

This article says men accused of crimes must be tried before the king's judges and not local magistrates. At the time, there was a lot of corruption and often local magistrates and judges were corrupt and harsh in rendering judgements.

Article 30:   "No sheriff or bailiff of ours, or any other person, shall take the horses or carts of any Freeman for transport against the will of the said freeman" (McKechnie 392).

Articles 28-31 deal with provisions forbidding bribery & official misconduct. Today we have laws against corruption to try and protect individuals.

Article 39:   "No freeman shall be arrested, or detained in prison or deprived of his freehold, or outlawed, or banished or in any way molested; and we will not set forth against him nor send against him, unless by the lawful judgement of his peers and by the law of the land" (McKechnie 436).

This article was a promise of law and liberty and good government to everyone. Specifically, it guaranteed trial by jury to all Englishmen. Furthermore, this article forbade King John from placing execution before judgement. Our founding fathers believed whole-heartedly in this concept of due process and equality before the law.

Years later, they included these concepts in the *United States Bill of Rights, Amendment V*. More on this later.

Article 45: "We will appoint as justices, constables, sheriffs, or bailiffs, only such as know the Law of the realm and mean to observe it well."
(McKechnie 440).

This too is interesting. In 1215, Englishmen realized the importance of appointing qualified individuals to do a job. Eventually Americans would take this concept and create civil service jobs today.

Article 60: "Moreover, all the aforesaid customs and liberties, the observance of which we have Granted in our kingdom as far as pertains to us towards our men, shall be observed By all of our kingdom, as well clergy as laymen, as far as pertains to them towards their men." (McKechnie 543).

Herein we see the development of a document to serve as the law of the land. Later, our founding fathers will create several documents that were to serve as the laws of our land.

Article 63: "The English Church shall be free and that men in the kingdom shall also have their Liberties, rights and concessions" (Barrington).

Years later this concept shows up in the writings of John Locke and also in the *U.S. Bill of Rights, Amendment I.*
(The idea of separation of Church and State).

You might think our story ends there but it doesn't. English history teaches us monarchs tried to retain as much of their absolute power as possible for the longest time, despite a democratic parliamentary system of government which began to develop in England following the *Magna Carta.*

Unfortunately, trouble developed in England because of the development of Parliamentary government. The members of Parliament over time, tried to assert their right to make important legal decisions in the realm, regardless of the king's wishes. More and more they attempted to codify (put into writing) some of the important human and civil rights they had forced prior kings to accept like in the *Magna Carta.*

King Charles I, son of James I, wanted none of this. He whole heartedly believed in the Theory of Divine Right. He did not see a need for a Parliament, nor did he want a Parliament questioning his judgement. After all, he had been chosen by God to be the King of England.

Things came to a head during the reign of Charles I of England (1625-1649). Believing he had a royal-right, Charles I began to raise money by taxing his subjects in most unusual ways. Just to name a few, there were new custom duties, and ship money taxes. In addition, he took money from people in a process that became known as "Forced Loans" (King Charles I of England). All of this was done without the consent of Parliament.

British citizens, especially the nobility, became extremely alarmed with the king's abuse of power. And, it wasn't just a matter of taxation. Charles declared martial law in areas that were extremely agitated by these taxes as well as religious difficulties. Thus, he sent soldiers to keep order and in so doing required ordinary citizens to feed and house them. This was known as forced billets (King Charles I of England; The Civil War).

Parliament on the other hand did not believe Charles I had the power to do such things without their consent. Furthermore, Parliament probably believed these acts by the new king were in violation of clauses in the *Magna Carta*, which Englishmen had come to look upon as their civil liberties.

On June 15, 1628, Parliament drafted and presented to Charles I, a document, which became known as the "The Petition of Right." The purpose of this document was to solidify and to again codify (put in writing for all to read) English civil liberties and human rights. Below is a list of some of the main points of the *Petition of Right*.

III: "...And whereas also by the statute called 'The Great Charter of the Liberties of England,' it is declared and enacted, that no freeman may be taken or imprisoned or be disseized of his freehold or liberties, or his free customs, or be outlawed or exiled, or in any manner destroyed, but by the lawful judgment of his peers, or by the law of the land."

  This concept will show up years later in the *U.S. Bill of Rights, Amendment VI.*

IV: "...no man, of what estate or condition that he be, should be put out of his land or tenements, nor taken, nor imprisoned, nor disinherited nor put to death without being brought to answer by due process."

This concept will show up years later in the *U.S. Bill of Rights, Amendment V*.

VI: "...And whereas of late great companies of soldiers and mariners have been dispersed into counties of the realm, and the inhabitants against their wills have been compelled to receive them into their houses"

This concept will show up years later in the *U.S. Bill of Rights, Amendment III*.

X: "...no man hereafter be compelled to make or yield any gift, loan, benevolence, tax, or such like charge, without common consent by act of parliament; and that none be called to make answer, or take such oath, or to give attendance, or be confined, or otherwise molested or disquieted concerning the same or for refusal thereof; and that no freeman, in any such manner as is before mentioned, be imprisoned or detained; ...or put to death contrary to the laws and franchise of the land" (Roland).

This concept will show up years later in the *U.S. Bill of Rights, Amendment VIII*.

The Petition of Right was a complement to the Magna Carta. Essentially, the above articles declared that "Englishmen shall never be subject to martial law" (Smith 12).

In response to the petition, Charles I, in 1626, dissolved Parliament. He did not call for another Parliament for eleven years (King Charles I of England). This time period became known as the "Eleven Years Tyranny" because during that time period, the country was subject to despotism of the Privy Council, the Star Chamber, the Court of High Commission; in place of laws, proclamations;

in place of legal taxation by Parliament, forced loans, monopolies, feudal and forest extortions, ship money; the tenure of judges made during the king's pleasure, that they might be perfect slaves to the king's will and more took place (Smith 13).

After eleven years without a Parliament, King Charles I finally called for Parliamentary elections again in response to a Scottish rebellion over religion. That Parliament became known as the "Long Parliament." It lasted for twenty years. During that time, it resisted Charles I as best it could until finally in 1642, civil war broke out between the king and his forces versus those of Parliament (King Charles I of England).

The king's forces were known as the Cavaliers. They consisted of nobles, wealthy men and their supporters. Parliament's forces became known as the Roundheads. They favored a republican commonwealth over monarchy as the form of government for England. Also, the name Round Heads was derived from their hair style. Most of them were Puritans and as such dressed modestly and wore their hair short in contrast to the nobles who wore their hair long (Who Were the Roundheads).

The English Civil War raged for four long years and it was a terrible civil war. During that time Oliver Cromwell became the leader of the Parliamentary forces. He turned out to be a great military leader and eventually defeated and forced the king's army to dissolve in 1646.
Story over, right? …not in English history. Believe it or not, Charles I still refused to accept the power of Parliament to make and enforce laws. Also, Cromwell did not trust Charles I. Most likely, he believed as long as the king was alive, there was the possibility of a counter-revolution. Therefore, Cromwell, with the support of the army, forced over 100 delegates to leave Parliament (the Long Parliament shrunk from 500 members in 1640 to about 150 by 1649).

Now, only those members loyal to Cromwell remained. This Parliament became known as the "Rump Parliament." Subsequently, the Rump Parliament tried and condemned Charles I for treason. To make a long story short, Charles I was publicly executed on a scaffold by decapitation on 30 January 1649 (The Civil War & Charles I; Roland).

This was significant for two reasons. First, it was the first time a western European king had ever been executed. This act would set a precedent which years later would make it a bit easier for the French to execute King Louis XVI and Queen Marie Antoinette. Second, English civil liberties were safe, at least for the present.

As a result of all this chaos in England, the age-old debate about what is the best form of government reared its head again. In ancient times, the Greeks had experimented with democracy. This form of government can take different forms, but essentially it allows all citizens to participate in selecting the rulers to govern them. Later, the Romans picked up on this and created a type of representative democracy called a Republic, whereby power was vested in both elected representatives to a Senate and a leader or leaders who managed the empire. This didn't turn out so well for the Romans. Eventually, civil war broke out in 49-45 BC between the two leaders at the time...Julius Caesar and Pompey.

Unfortunately for Pompey, his legions were defeated by those of Julius Caesar and he (Pompey) was murdered by the Egyptians when he fled to Alexandria, Egypt.

After Julius Caesar's untimely murder in the Senate on the Ides of March, 15 March 44 BC., the empire took up an autocracy form of government. This meant all power was concentrated into the hands of one person who could pretty much do anything he wanted to do. That person was Octavian, who became the first Emperor of the Roman Empire. Such an arrangement many argued boded well for security and stability, which the Roman Empire had neither during the Democratic Republican phase of government.

This idea proved to be popular in the Middle Ages. Strong men ruled almost everywhere. But, during the Renaissance another form of government developed in the Italian city states. This became known as an Oligarchy form of government, which simply meant that power was vested in a few people, like a family (the Medici family and the Borgias are good examples) or a noble class. It never proved to be quite popular with the masses and in time, most noble classes in Europe became corrupt.

Nevertheless, for hundreds of years, kings with the help of the church and a noble class, ruled in Europe. This form of government was further solidified by the Theory of Divine Right. This theory began during the time of Henry VIII in England, who desperately needed to assert his right to break away from the Catholic Church in Europe so that he could divorce his wife and remarry in an effort to procreate an heir. The idea was that a king had absolute power on Earth to do what he or she wished because God had so ordained it. James I, in England, believed whole heartedly in this theory and promoted it throughout his realm during this lifetime (What is the Divine Right Theory of Government). He proclaimed to his subjects he had been appointed by God to rule and therefore was different than other men. He also believed all power was vested in him to rule. His decisions were binding on all his subjects. Even the nobles took a back seat and were now seen as those individuals who would help the king manage the realm.

The Divine Right Theory over the next few centuries became popular with monarchs all across Europe, until the French Revolution in 1789. Only in England was it seriously challenged before 1789. There, because of the signing of the *Magna Carta*, a history of parliamentary government began to rival that of the king's theory of Divine Right. As noted earlier, all this came to a head with The Petition of Right passed by Parliament and the ensuing English Civil War. And, after the public execution of Charles I, people began to search for answers again about what would be the best form of government for England to adopt. Numerous people wrote about the nature of man and political theory and what type of government was needed by a country to provide security and stability for its people.

Eventually, two men emerged who would not only influence European politics but English politics forever. In time, they also influence our founding fathers years later.

The first man was Thomas Hobbes, who two years after Charles I was executed, published his political thoughts and ideas in a book titled, "Leviathan", 1651. A Leviathan was a kind of mythical, all powerful monster, (Student Bible, Job 41 749-750). Some highlights of his ideas are as follows:

- It is hard for people to govern themselves because they have difficulty working together. In a natural state…"men live without a common Power to keep them all in awe, they are in that condition which is called Warre; and such a warre, as is of every man, against every man. Also, in this state of Warre, there is no time for industry, navigation, nor commodities that may be imported by sea; no commodious Building; no instruments of moving, no knowledge of the Earth; no account of Time; no Arts; no Letters; no Society; …only continual fear, and danger of violent death; And the life of man, solitary, poor, nasty, brutish, and short" (Hobbes 185-186).
- A civilized society can only be obtained if a government/ruler ("a Common Power") has complete

authority to rule. In other words, "a Common Power may be able to defend them (the multitude) from the invasion of foreigners, and the injuries of one another." This Common Power is "made by Covenant (a social contract) of every man with every man, I Authorize and give up my Right of Governing myself, to this Man, (a king/monarch) or to this Assembly of men (a parliament), on this condition, that thou give up thy Right to him, and Authorize all his Actions in like manner. This is the Generation of that great LEVIATHAN...For by this Authorities given to him (a king), he has the use of so much Power and Strength conferred on him, that by terror thereof, he is not able to form the wills of them all, to Peace at home

Vera & Viva Effigies THOMÆ HOBBES Malmesburiensis

Image from the National Gallery in Prague

Thomas Hobbes
(1588-1679)

and against their enemies abroad. Government must be like a kind of Leviathan in order to provide peace, order and Stability" (Hobbes 227).

- Furthermore, it was dangerous for anyone to question the actions of their king because it could lead to chaos and possibly, a return to a state of Warre. "And therefore, they that are subjects to a Monarch, cannot without his leave cast off Monarchy, and return to the confusion of a disunited Multitude" (Hobbes 229).

Clearly, from Hobbes' writings, we can see the impact on him of the English Civil war. The day Charles I was publicly executed, was perhaps, one of the worst days in Hobbes life.

John Locke, another English political philosopher also lived during the English Civil War. He disagreed somewhat with Hobbes. His ideas tended to favor a Parliamentary (democratic) form of government. Some of his ideas were published in "Two Treatises of Government," published in 1690 to justify the Glorious Revolution of 1688-1689. They included:

- There is an equality of men in nature. All men are in a state of perfection, freedom to order their actions. The Laws of Nature desire the peace and preservation of all mankind (Locke 167-169).

Image from the Library of Congress

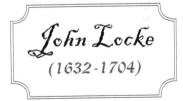

John Locke
(1632-1704)

- Despite the desire for peace and preservation, a state of War may occur. When this happens, the Fundamental Law of Nature says the safety of the individual is to be preserved: And one may destroy a man who makes war upon him for the same reason he may kill a wolf or a lion (Locke 177).

- People possess by nature certain human rights which do not belong to the state (any government). "The natural liberty of man is to be free from any superior power on Earth, and not to be under the will or legislative authority of man but to have only the law of nature as his rule. The Liberty of man in Society, is to be under no other legislative power, but that established by consent in the Commonwealth, nor under the Dominion of any Will, or restraint of any Law, but what the legislative shall enact, according to the trust put in it." Property is another right mankind possesses. Locke referred to these rights as inalienable rights, the right to **life**, **liberty**, and **property** (Locke 182; 184-202).

- In order to protect their inalienable rights, men agree to establish a government. Furthermore, a government is based on a kind of contract created by people and their ruler. "Men join and unite into a community, for their comfortable, safe and peaceable living one amongst another, in a secure enjoyment of their properties and a greater security against any that are not of it" (Locke 238).

- "The great ends of men entering into society, being the enjoyment of their properties in Peace and Safety and the great instrument and means of that being the laws established in society: The First and Fundamental law of all Commonwealths, is the establishing of the Legislative Power; as the first and fundamental natural law, which is to govern the legislative in itself, is the preservation of society and every person in it" (Locke 267).

- "Thus that learned king who well understood the notions of things, makes the difference betwixt a King and a Tyrant to consist only in this, The one makes the Laws the Bounds of his Power, and the Good of the Public, the end of his government; the other makes all give way to his own Will and Appetite. Where-ever Law ends, Tyranny begins, if the Law be transgressed to another's harm" (Locke 322-323).

- "The reason why men enter into society is the preservation of their property...whenever the legislators endeavor to take away, and destroy the Property of the People, or to reduce them to slavery under Arbitrary Power, they put themselves into a state of war with the people, who thereupon absolved from any farther obedience, and are left to the common Refuge, which God hath provided for all Men, against force and Violence" (Locke, 337). Here is where Locke is saying if a government fails to protect people's inalienable rights, they have the right to dissolve that government.

Fast forward to the 1770s in the thirteen English colonies in North America. You can bet, almost to a man, our founding fathers read and studied the ideas of Hobbes and Locke. However, it was Locke's ideas they embraced the most. No doubt most founding fathers had a copy of Locke's, *Two Treatises on Government*, in their library collection of books or they had studied Locke's ideas in their formal education. Either way, it is with Locke where we begin to understand what it means to be an American today.

After ten years of futile petitions to George III in England, our founding fathers turned to Locke, who believed if a government failed to protect people's inalienable rights (life, liberty and property), then the governed (the people), had a right to rebel against its government. Our founding fathers came to the same conclusion. In addition, they began to see King George III as a tyrant. Thus, they sent representatives to Philadelphia, PA, from every colony in 1776, to discuss the momentous decision of separation from the mother country.

In a sense, when Americans arrived in Philadelphia, PA in 1776, they were already unique in the world. They knew about and believed in Locke's ideas and in the ideas of the Enlightenment, those human rights and civil liberties. The only problem at that time was their king, George III did not. In petition after petition, colonial leaders persevered to try and convince English King George III to agree to as many of them as possible. Unfortunately, George III had little interest in changing the system. He too believed in the Theory of Divine Right and failed to understand the argument regarding government participation by the Americans. Because of this, Americans began to view George III as a tyrant who was not fulfilling his part of the social contract made with his people. Americans felt he had not only abused their rights to property but at times tortured people, imprisoned them without just cause, and even executed them without a trial by jury. Furthermore, Americans most likely began to view the noble class in England as immoral because of their support for George III and his policies. It is not a coincidence that years later, when the constitution was written, a provision was put in to guarantee there would never be a noble class in America.

Article I, Section 9 of the Constitution

"No title of Nobility shall be granted by the United States: And no Person holding any Office of Profit or Trust under them, shall, without the Consent of Congress, accept of any present, Emolument, Office or Title, of any kind whatever, from any King, Prince or foreign State" (Declaration of Independence: A Transcription).

By 1776, no one was safe in the colonies. Independence for many seemed like the only sensible alternative left. The discussions in the thirteen original colonies now went from debate to about how government should work to serious talk of establishing a new government in America for Americans. That government most believed should be based on Locke's ideas of Life, Liberty and Property. Furthermore, people began to talk of other Enlightenment ideas, human rights and civil liberties being incorporated into a new government, free from king George III in England. All thirteen colonies bought into this concept and sent delegates to Philadelphia in the summer of 1776 to discuss the matter.

Upon arriving in Philadelphia, in June of 1776, a committee was formed to rough out a separation document that could be read to the American people and ultimately sent to king George III in England. This committee was composed of Benjamin Franklin from Pennsylvania, John Adams from Massachusetts, Roger Sherman from Connecticut, Robert Livingston from New York, and Thomas Jefferson from Virginia.

Early on, it was decided Thomas Jefferson would rough out the separation document for review with input from members of the committee. Thus, after much discussion among committee members, Jefferson incorporated many of John Locke's political ideas in this separation document.

Jefferson finished the document and presented it to the delegates at the convention in Philadelphia on 3 July 1776. The separation document was voted on (democracy) by the delegates...it passed and was then signed by most of the delegates. After the signing it was read to the people of Philadelphia on July 4th, 1776, followed by ringing the "Liberty Bell."

Known as *The Declaration of Independence*, this important American document spelled out why the thirteen colonies were declaring their freedom to the world. It was also the beginning of another civil war between Englishmen, so to speak. This conflict became known as the American Revolutionary War.

Volumes have been written about the American Revolutionary War. There is even a museum dedicated to the war today in Philadelphia, PA. However, what history often overlooks are the important ideas that colonists were willing to fight for and die for, if necessary…the ones Jefferson included in *The Declaration of Independence*. These ideas were in fact what people everywhere in the thirteen colonies were willing to risk everything for, including their honor and their life! So, let's begin our understanding of what it means to be an American by looking at some of these important ideas in *The Declaration of Independence*.

What Does it mean to be an American?

$\mathfrak{C}$ hapter 1

1776
The Declaration of Independence

If you have not read *The Declaration of Independence*, you should do so. It is an incredible document. Incorporated into this document are ideas from Locke and other Enlightenment philosophes (writers who championed reform and advocated toleration in society and government in the 18th century). Below are some of the main points and ideas. Individually these ideas are impressive but the synergy of them all together makes *The Declaration of Independence* a masterpiece in the history of mankind. It also made the people living in the thirteen colonies uniquely American in the eyes of the world.

Paragraph 1

The stage is set. It tells the world Americans have the right to declare independence, that we are going to separate from England and why (the causes) which drove us to declare our independence.

"When in the Course of human events, it becomes necessary for one people to dissolve the political bands which have connected them with another, and to assume among the powers of the earth, the separate and equal station to which the Laws of Nature and of Nature's God entitle them, a decent respect to the opinions of mankind requires that they should declare the causes which impel them to the separation" (Declaration of Independence: A Transcription).

Paragraph 2

"All men are created equal"
(Declaration of Independence: A Transcription)

Here we have one of the great ideas of humankind. It goes back as far as passages in the Bible. If you search the internet for this phrase, you will see references which quote Bible passages which lend themselves to this theme. Also, during the Enlightenment, philosophes like Locke spoke of equality for mankind. Locke wrote:

> "All mankind...being all equal and independent, no one ought to harm another in his life, liberty, or possessions" (property) (Landrum).

Jefferson took Locke's ideas and somewhat changed his ideas on what are unalienable Rights.

"Unalienable Rights"
(Declaration of Independence: A Transcription)

What exactly are unalienable Rights? Most likely most Americans in 1776 had never heard of unalienable Rights. Fortunately, many of the founding fathers, especially Thomas Jefferson, understood them quite well. He knew, as Locke had said, that unalienable Rights were natural laws that come from God. As such, every human being was entitled to them. In addition, people could not be denied these unalienable rights by a government nor could they be taken away by anyone on this Earth. Therefore, neither king George nor the English government could deprive or deny any American of unalienable Rights.

Specifically, these Rights included, according to Locke, the Right to Life, the Right to Liberty and the Right to Property. Jefferson wholeheartedly believed in all three of them. However, when he wrote *The Declaration of Independence*, he changed the last unalienable Right. He wrote:

> "We hold these truths to be self-evident that all men are created equal, that they are endowed by their Creator with certain **unalienable Rights**, that among these are **Life, Liberty and the pursuit of Happiness**" (Declaration of Independence: A Transcription).

People in the thirteen colonies already believed they had the right to own property. So, instead of using the word property, Jefferson changed the third Right to "the pursuit of Happiness" (Declaration of Independence: A Transcription). It made all the difference in the world. That one change transformed *The Declaration of Independence* from a discussion on political differences to something so powerful and uniquely American, that seemingly almost everyone in the colonies bought into it.

"The Right to Life"
(Declaration of Independence: A Transcription)

Why did John Locke list this as the first unalienable right? Well, even in 1776 when kings believed in Divine Right, terrible atrocities were often committed by kings and their ministers/governments. In short, no one's life was safe. If a king believed you had said bad things about him or his family, he could have you tortured, imprisoned, or even executed. Your estate (property) could have been forfeited to the crown and the king would have re-distributed it to a more "loyal" family.

Because of this, several ideas were formulated throughout time in Europe and ultimately in America to protect a person's life. We saw this concept in the Magna Carta and again in the Petition of Right and in Locke's writings. Finally, it shows up in the second paragraph of *The Declaration of Independence* as the first unalienable Right.

Image from the Library of Congress

Jean-Jacques Rousseau
(1712-1778)

"Liberty"
(Declaration of Independence: A Transcription)

Here again we see the influence of John Locke, but we also see the influence of Jean Jacques Rousseau (1712-1778), who 1n 1762, in the *Social Contract*, wrote, "man is born free and everywhere he is in chains" (Rousseau, chapter 1). Rousseau, like Locke, believed man was in the state of nature, basically good. However, problems arise when mankind becomes corrupted.

Perhaps if we could have talked with Rousseau, he would have agreed that kings and their governments often become corrupted in their quest to hold onto power and to accumulate wealth for themselves. Society too can become corrupt. The noble class for the most part prior to the French Revolution is a great example of this. They had stacked the deck against everyone else, so to speak, to maintain their wealth for not only themselves but for their heirs. It was very difficult for ordinary people who were not of noble birth in France to raise their status in society and to enjoy a bit of the good life for themselves and their families. Essentially, there was little liberty for mankind in a society like this.

When Jefferson wrote of liberty, he envisioned a society where people would be free to voice their opinions without fear of punishment. Free to move and live wherever they wished. Free to live their life as they wished...not to be pressed into military service at any time. Freedom meant many things to many people living in the thirteen English colonies which declared independence from England in 1776. It was something most of them were willing to fight for.

Unfortunately, Jefferson's idea of liberty didn't really mean freedom for all. By 1776, slavery had been institutionalized in the thirteen colonies, especially in the southern colonies. And, despite the fact Jefferson wrote "all men are created equal" (Declaration of Independence: A Transcription) in *The Declaration of Independence*, there was little concerted effort in early America to free the slaves. It was not until the American Civil War that slavery was finally outlawed in America. It took the life of almost one million people to resolve this and thereafter, amendments to the *Constitution of the United States*. Today, despite the constant struggle against racism, almost all human beings should believe in this enlightenment idea, especially in terms of laws and social justice/culture.

Liberty also referred to states' rights. This debate raged in 1776, it raged during the American Civil War and it still rears its head in occasional political discussions today. The fact is, States are not totally free to do whatever they wish. In the *Constitution of the United States of America*, certain powers are given to the federal government while others are reserved for the states. For example, each state is free to educate their youth, for the most part, as they see fit. In fact, in most states public education is governed by a state education code.

In addition, there are rights that both the federal government and states have simultaneously. These powers are called concurrent powers. Taxation is an example of a concurrent power. Both the federal government and individual states, if they so choose, can tax an individual's personal income. More on taxes later.

So, you see we are not free to do as we please whenever we please. We cannot, for example, break a law without being held accountable for those actions. But we are free in a multitude of ways. In fact, people have more freedom in America than in many other countries around the world. And we as Americans love the fact, we have so much freedom.

"The Pursuit of Happiness"
(Declaration of Independence: A Transcription)

Our last unalienable Right also comes from Locke. However, Jefferson changed it, as mentioned before, from property to "the pursuit of Happiness." Most likely, the right to own property (Locke's third unalienable right), was by 1776 an implied right that all Englishmen believed in. Or perhaps things were so miserable right before *The Declaration of Independence*, that Jefferson felt inclined to change it to "the pursuit of Happiness."

This change had profound implications. It means that people are free to try and build a life for their families based on love and happiness. Common sense, yes…yet in 1776, people were not always free to do these things.

Today, social questions such as healthcare can be inferred in Unalienable Rights. If people cannot afford to buy healthcare or are unable to get a basic healthcare program for themselves and their families, then the question arises, can they really pursue happiness? If you say no to that question, then our society and government needs to strive to provide everyone with some type of basic healthcare program in order to pursue happiness.

A Social Contract does exist between People and a Government

Both Hobbes and Locke spoke of a social contract between people and government. The difference is on what happens when that social contract is violated. For Hobbes, he would probably say you cannot dissolve that contract because ordinary people are not capable of governing themselves. Ordinary people are inherently "quarrelsome and turbulent." Locke, on the other hand, believed people could govern themselves and when a government fails to protect those unalienable Rights, people are free to dissolve the government.

People have a right to break that social contract and establish a new government

Again, it was Locke who won the day with founding fathers on this subject. We can see this in the second paragraph of *The Declaration of Independence*. Jefferson wrote,

"Governments are instituted among Men, deriving their just powers from the consent of the governed, - That whenever any Form of Government, becomes destructive of these ends, it is the Right of the People to alter or to abolish it, and to institute new Government laying its foundation on such principles and organizing its powers in such form, as to them shall seem most likely to affect their Safety and Happiness" (Declaration of Independence: A Transcription).

He goes on to talk about people not changing the government on a whim. Dissolving or changing a government is not something to take lightly. However, if governmental abuses become unbearable, leading people to believe it is absolute Despotism, then people have a right to change it. "It is the right, it is their duty, to throw off such Government, and to provide new Guards for their future security" (Declaration of Independence: A Transcription).

Jefferson goes on to outline about twenty-seven abuses by king George III and his government which gave the American colonies the right to dissolve the link between them and England. Some of these abuses were eventually addressed in the *Constitution of the United States* and became American values which we still believe in today.

The Enlightenment concepts in *The Declaration of Independence* gave Americans more than hope. They gave Americans the motivation and the power to sustain a long and bloody civil war against the mother country. The result was independence and the creation of a new country that would become the envy of the world.

Chapter 2

1781
The Articles of Confederation

On June 7, 1776, in anticipation of the eventual *Declaration of Independence*, Virginia delegate Richard Henry Lee moved to establish a committee for the purpose of developing a written document that would serve as a new government for the thirteen colonies. Later in committee, John Dickenson from Pennsylvania put forward some solid ideas on how this new government would function. These ideas proved to be controversial. Thus, during the war years, July 4th, 1776 until 1781, the Continental Congress debated what type of government our new country would need. A similar debate was also occurring in the thirteen colonies.

These debates were contentious. On the one hand, the might and military power of the mother country was ever present. Even if the war could be won, England's power posed an ongoing threat to America. It was this threat that made a union with all thirteen colonies a necessity. Yet, the problem was however, each state had developed independent of one another and was leery of any kind of union being formed that would be strong and autocratic like England. Each state wanted to maintain as much of a great degree of independence as possible yet be bound together for safety from England or anybody else for that matter. It was this believe in having as much independence as possible for each state that tended to obstruct and hinder the needed consolidation for our new country (Ridpath 349).

What an interesting time period this was for everyone. The Continental Army was somehow surviving and at times holding its own against British Regulars who were, the finest army in the world. In the Continental Congress, representatives were working together in the interest of unity to try and resolve not only military challenges but other pressing problems as well. There were financial challenges regarding arms and munitions and cannons for the war efforts. There were food challenges...an army has to eat. There were land challenges. One such challenge was what to do with western lands once the war was over. Virginia had previously laid claim to much of these lands, but other states also wanted to allow their citizens to expand into these territories. Lastly, there was the question of what type of government our new country would adopt. We will discuss the land questions later but for now, let's examine where the ideas came from for the *Articles of Confederation.*

Much has been written by scholars about the origins of and the type of government structure the *Articles of Confederation* would take. In Richard B. Bernstein's book, ARE WE TO BE A NATION? The making of *The Constitution*, he theorized prior attempts at colonial union gave rise to specific American ideas of government. These included, "a written constitution, doctrine of separation of powers, a declaration of rights, and the constitutional and ratifying conventions (Bernstein 43)." Let's add one more idea to those, that of a confederacy type of government. It was this idea that gave rise to a serious debate among American scholars.

As far back as 1744 at a treaty conference at the Lancaster County Court House, in Lancaster, PA, one of the attending Iroquois chiefs by the name of Canasatego, recommended to the colonists, they develop a union like the Iroquois Confederation. Such a union would yield advantages including a strong friendship between the colonies as well as the Iroquois Confederation. Canasatego related how establishing their confederation gave the Iroquois "great Weight and Authority with our neighboring nations"(Colden 200). He went on to say that now, "we are a powerful Confederacy; and, by your observing the same Methods our wise forefathers have taken, you will acquire fresh strength and power" (Colden 200). It is interesting to note, founding Father Benjamin Franklin was in attendance that day in Lancaster and seemed impressed by Canasatego's words (Payne 609).

Ten years later, in 1754 another Iroquois chief, Hendrick, also recommended the colonies form a union. The meeting with leaders of the Iroquois Confederacy was held in Albany, NY with representatives from the colonies attending. During the meeting Hendrick spoke of the structure of the Iroquois league. When Hendrick was done speaking, Benjamin Franklin proposed the colonies join together in a similar type of union. Franklin's plan was called the Albany Plan of Union. Upon discussion of the union plan, a few changes were made to Franklin's ideas, but the plan was adopted by the representatives. Unfortunately, when the representatives returned home, they were unable to sway their colonial legislatures. The Albany Plan of Union was not adopted by the legislatures (Payne 610).

Two other events occurred before the *Declaration of Independence* which lead some scholars to believe Native Americans did play a role in influencing the founding fathers in their challenge to develop a national government. First, Benjamin Franklin submitted a draft of the *Articles of Confederation* to the Continental Congress July 21, 1775. Some argued the draft of the *Articles of Confederation* was based on the Albany Plan which was rejected years earlier.

A month later, national unity was discussed at a treaty conference between Iroquois leaders and the Continental Congress, August 24-September 1, 1775. Could it be Franklin wanted the Iroquois leaders in town to answer any questions about their confederation? Then in June and July of 1776, twenty-one Iroquois leaders visited Philadelphia to meet with the Continental Congress (Payne 610). Many of their leaders were present when the Liberty Bell was rung, and *The Declaration of Independence* was read and distributed to the people of Philadelphia. Could it be that in the Iroquois Confederation, the founding fathers found some of their answers to the problem of how to unify and protect themselves while at the same time allowing each colony to enjoy a great degree of independence?

Of course, every legitimate coin has two sides. And on the flip side of this coin are the scholars who argue Native Americans had little influence on our founding fathers in their development of the *Articles of Confederation*. More importantly, when you read some of the comments of a few founding fathers you begin to realize the subject of race also played a role. Benjamin Franklin had studied Indian culture for years and was constantly involved with native Americans in various treaty conference. He most assuredly was not a racist. And to think he was not influenced by native American culture and political organization is simply not believable.

However, others felt native Americans had little to offer civilized Europeans. What could people living in the woods bring to the table when it came to organizing a new government. This discussion brings back shades of the Imperialism Period in Europe (1888-1914) whereby the Europeans' world view was laced with racism. It caused them to carve up Africa and parts of southeast Asia by 1914, because they believed only they could bring civilization to these areas.

The intent of this book is not to rehash the Imperialism Period in history or racism in America or Europe. However, we must leave open the possibility that racism influenced some of the founding fathers in the development of a union for the Thirteen Colonies. And because of this people would argue the *Articles of Confederation* were developed after studying historical European confederacies like Ancient Greece, the Achean League, the Holy Roman Empire, Poland, the Swiss Confederacy, and the United Provinces of the Netherlands (Payne 618).

However, it seems that it is only logical that native Americans did influence the development of our first written government. Racism did not win the day. On the contrary, founding fathers like Benjamin Franklin understood the important concepts found in native American cultures and past colonial experiments in creating a union between the colonies like the ideas proposed in 1751 by Benjamin Franklin for a colonial union strictly for defense. Franklin also expanded on his ideas and published them in the Pennsylvania Gazette in 1754. He called his plan "Short Hints" and brought it to Albany for discussion that same year (Bernstein). And while his plan was adopted in Albany by the delegates sent to the conference, the individual States never agreed to the plan.

Despite this rejection, the search continued for a government style that could work but would not be a copy of what England practiced. This search during the Second Continental Congress led some of our founding fathers to the Iroquois Confederation. In this native American organization, our founding fathers were able to see various English philosophical concepts, like those of John Locke (Life, Liberty and Property) put into a practical form of government which would give the colonists the protection they desired while at the same time giving each colony a great deal of independence. Other important political concepts adopted by our founding fathers included the rights of people to give their consent to be governed rather than being coerced by an autocratic government. In addition, some scholars believe native Americans further influenced our founding fathers in the development of many political concepts about how to govern like checks and balances, religious toleration, no state church, federalism, equal rights before the law, the impeachment of government officials, and even issues concerning women's rights (Payne, 607). Thus, it seems reasonable to conclude that many of these political philosophical ideas which enlightenment philosophes in Europe had written about were already being practiced in some way in the Iroquois Confederation. Perhaps knowing this made it a bit easier for the founding fathers to step out on the limb when it came to putting their synthesized ideas into practice in the form of the *Articles of Confederation*.

Thus, the question of whether or not the *Articles of Confederation* was truly influenced by native Americans was answered by the United States Congress in 1988. The U.S. Congress that year passed a resolution stating, "the *Articles of Confederation* was influenced by the political system developed by the Iroquois Confederation (Payne, 606)." This is not to say the details were exactly like those found in the Iroquois Confederation. On the contrary, the details of how the new government would work was most likely a product of research done on European historical confederacies synthesized with political philosophies of the day in the hopes of creating something new and different in America, something that would be much different than in England.

The details of how the new confederation would function were finally discovered on November 15, 1777, when the Continental Congress voted and reluctantly adopted the *Articles of Confederation*. This was America's first government with a written document. Furthermore, the name adopted for our new nation was continued (Congress renames the nation "United States of America"). In Article I it stated: "the style of this confederacy shall be 'The United States of America'" (Articles of Confederation Transcript). Over the next few years, one by one, all thirteen colonies approved and ratified the *Articles of Confederation*. The last two states to do so were Delaware in February of 1779 and lastly, Maryland in March of 1781 (Ridpath 349-351).

Shortly thereafter, in October 1781, the war came to a head. The British army in the south led by Lord Cornwallis had been bottled up on the Yorktown peninsula by General Washington and the Continental Army with the help of a French army assisting the Americans led by Lieutenant General Rochambeau. Most likely, Lord Cornwallis initially wasn't too worried at the time. He had sent for a British fleet of ships to evacuate his troops and carry them safely back to New York to live to fight another day. Can you imagine the look on his face when he was informed the British fleet would not be arriving any time soon? A French Fleet, under the command of Admiral DeGrasse, had engaged and defeated the British fleet in the Chesapeake Bay area, thus forcing the British to turn their fleet around and head back to New York without Lord Cornwallis and his troops (Abrams). The rest is history. The Americans won a great victory at Yorktown. Lord Cornwallis was so upset he refused to attend the surrender ceremony. His adjutant, at first, tried to give the surrender sword to Lieutenant General Rochambeau. He refused to accept it and directed Cornwallis' adjutant to give the surrender sword to General Washington.

With the war winding down, the path was set to move toward peace and negotiations ending the American Revolutionary War. All attention was turned toward governing our new nation.

The Continental Congress was our first attempt at governing. However, it was never meant to be the vehicle by which we would permanently govern America. In June of 1776, a representative to the Second Continental Congress, Richard Henry Lee, as it was later reported in the Journals of the Continental Congress proposed the following resolution. "Resolved, That these United Colonies are, and of right ought to be, free and independent States, that they are absolved from all allegiance to the British Crown, and that all political connection between them and the State of Great Britain is, and ought to be, totally dissolved. That it is expedient forthwith to take the most effectual measures for forming foreign Alliances. That a plan of confederation be prepared and transmitted to the respective Colonies for their consideration and approbation" (Lee 425). Note the second part of Lee's resolution was to adopt "a plan of confederation [to] be prepared and transmitted to the respective Colonies for their consideration and approbation." It took several years but this plan turned out to be the *Articles of Confederation* later ratified by the respective Colonies. This was America's second attempt at governing, that would serve as a roadmap going forward. This document was a "sort of democratic republic...a form of a loose union of independent commonwealths...a confederation of sovereign states" (Ridpath 351). As it turned out, a loose confederation of the independent commonwealths had won the day, for now, over the argument for a strong federal government.

Upon examining the articles, one could say the founding fathers believed the spirit of cooperation would carry the day as it had during the war years. The only problem was during the war years it was essential for everyone to cooperate if they wanted to win. After the war that was not the case. Individual State interests seemed at times to dominate political discussions in Congress. Furthermore, the design of the *Articles of Confederation* made it downright difficult at times to govern and grow. The characteristics of the *Articles of Confederation* itself proved to be a source of frustration for our new government, especially when it came to providing our new nation with needed goods and services.

Some of the provisions of this loosely confederated government eventually became a source of frustration. They included:

- **No permanent President**
  (no chief executive branch of government).

    However, when Congress was not in session, the articles called for "A Committee of the States" to manage the day to day operations of the government. This committee consisted on one delegate from each state. And, "one of their number to preside" as a President. This individual was not allowed "to serve in the office of President more than one year in any term of three years" (Articles of Confederation Transcript, Article IX).

    Can you imagine how difficult it must have been to run the entire government by committees or with a President who could only serve for a short time. Today our President serves as a type of CEO managing all cabinet positions and agencies throughout the government. Every day the President makes decisions that can affect millions of people. In addition, coordination is important to make things run more efficiently. How would you do that by committees? Obviously, things got done. But most likely it wasn't often coordinated nor was it efficient.

- **No national courts.**

Each state developed their own separate court system. You can imagine how this led to many challenges for people who moved between states doing business. In one state a judge might have ruled one way and in another state another judge countermanded that ruling. Thus, you had thirteen different legal systems developing, each with its own goals and motivations.

There was, however, under Article IV, a provision for extradition of criminals to another state. "If any person guilty of or charged with treason, felony, or other high misdemeanor in any state shall flee from justice, and be found in any of the United States, he shall, upon demand of the governor or executive power of the state from which he fled, be delivered up and removed to the state having jurisdiction of this offense" (Transcription of Articles of Confederation, Article IV). This provision would also show up in the United States Constitution years later.

- **No direct representation of people.**

The *Articles of Confederation* contradicted the doctrines outlined in *The Declaration of Independence*. The power of Congress was no more than a shadow. And, that shadow instead of being derived directly from the people, emanated from the States, which had declared themselves to be sovereign and independent (Ridpath 352).

Congress represented State governments. Furthermore, delegates were chosen by the state legislatures to represent their state in Congress. Under Article V, "No state shall be represented in Congress by less than two nor by more than seven members; and no person shall be capable of being a delegate for more than three years in any term of six years; nor shall any person, being a delegate, be capable of holding any office under the United States for which he, or another for his benefit, receives any salary, fees, or emolument of any kind" (Transcription of Articles of Confederation, Article V).

Here is a very interesting idea. From the beginning our founding fathers recognized the importance of having term limits for legislators. Somehow, this became lost years later when they drafted and ratified the new constitution. It is also interesting to note they did not want any delegate double dipping. You could not be a delegate and at the same time be paid to hold an official office. Clearly, they wanted the delegates to concentrate on doing what was right for our country. They were not there to profit for themselves in any way. This idea of sacrificing your time and energy on behalf of your country also has gotten lost in the modern world.

Representatives were also not chosen based on the population of that state. So, little Rhode Island had the same representation as a larger state like Virginia or Pennsylvania or New York. Seems odd given our set up today.

- Also, whether a state sent two or seven representatives to Congress, each state had only one vote.

"In determining questions in the United States in Congress assembled, each state shall have one vote" (Transcription of Articles of Confederation, Article V). Most likely a State delegation voted among themselves before they cast their single vote on any matter before Congress.

- Congress could raise money to support an army, but states had to agree to fund such an undertaking. This resulted in having no permanent armed forces. However, each state could maintain a militia for its defense.

"All charges of war and all other expenses that shall be incurred for the common defense or general welfare, and allowed by the United States in Congress assembled, shall be defrayed out of a common treasury, which shall be supplied by the several states in proportion to the value of all land within each state. Furthermore, the taxes for paying that proportion shall be laid and levied by the authority and direction of the legislatures of the several states within the time agreed upon by the United States in Congress assembled" (Transcription of Articles of Confederation, Article VIII).

This provision in particular must have been scary as hostilities had ceased but the war was technically not over. Northern forts, such as Fort Oswego, Fort Niagara, Fort Oswegatchie, Fort Pointe-au-Fer (all the aforementioned in New York state), Fort Dutchman's Point (in Vermont), Fort Detroit and Fort Michilmackinac (Michigan state) on American soil/western territory were still occupied by British soldiers after 1787 despite treaty provisions. The British justified the occupation of these forts on the premises the American's still had not re-payed debts owed to British subjects nor had they paid Loyalists for confiscation of their lands during/after the American Revolutionary War (Graebner 198-199; Longley). The Americans had no standing army, so it was difficult to recapture these forts without the financial support of all the states in raising another federal army.

In addition, you can see from the provisions laid out in the articles how time consuming and difficult it was to raise money. What if a state or two or three decided not to levy the taxes to raise the money to pay for such undertakings? Can you imagine in our modern world how things would have gone if we would have had to wait until the states raised money in order to respond to the Japanese attack on Pearl Harbor, December 7th, 1941? The bottom line is our new country had little money to respond immediately to problems let alone to pay British subjects for confiscated property.

- **Freedom of Speech.**

Here we see the foundation laid for the *Bill of Rights* years later. Clearly this was important to our founding fathers. Also, delegates could not be indicted for a crime while Congress was in session, unless it was a serious crime.

"Freedom of speech and debate in Congress shall not be impeached or questioned in any court or place out of Congress, and the members shall be protected in their persons from arrests and imprisonments during the time of their going to and from, and attendance on Congress, except for treason, felony, or breach of the peace" (Transcription of Articles of Confederation, Article V).

Today, many debates occur whether our President can be indicted while in office. Apparently, our founding fathers initially would have said yes if the crime was treason, a felony (a crime committed), or a breach of the peace!

- **Congress could borrow money if need be.**

That wasn't a problem. As stated earlier, the challenge was how to raise the money to repay any loans. In addition, given our new government structure and the difficulties we were having in repaying France for assistance during the Revolutionary War, countries were probably a bit cautious in loaning the United States money for any reason.

America's difficulties in repaying loans, especially to France, gets really interesting. Because King Louis XVI helped the colonists in their quest for independence, his treasury was on the verge of bankruptcy. Thus, just one year after the convention to reform the *Articles of Confederation* was called in May of 1787 in America, king Louis XVI called for the Estates General to meet the following year. This deliberative body, which had the power to enact new laws/taxes, etc., hadn't been called in 200 years. The purpose of the meeting was to reform the tax code so Louis XVI could raise more money through new taxes. Instead, when the delegates arrived in Paris, all over France, they brought with them a host of grievances and reform ideas they wanted to see enacted. Unfortunately for Louis XVI, things got out of control rapidly and the French Revolution was on!

- **Thus, other nations began to doubt if they could deal with the new United States for fear of not being repaid** any debts owed. Because Congress did not have the power to levy taxes, they were also dependent on whatever financial help States could provide to pay soldiers who served in the Revolutionary War.

This proved extremely ineffective. In fact, it led in one instance to an outright rebellion.

• **Shay's Rebellion 1786.**

Disgruntled soldier farmers who had been paid little for their war efforts were by 1786 suffering from high taxes and foreclosures on their properties. One such soldier, Daniel Shay, began to rally other ex-soldiers/farmers to protest. These protests eventually erupted into a full-blown rebellion. Unfortunately, Shay and his band of disgruntled soldiers/farmers went about the countryside burning local government court houses and other government properties. It took a military confrontation to put down the rebellion (Shay's Rebellion). It also emphasized the need for a stronger federal government, perhaps one with a standing army. On the eve of the Constitutional Convention, four states had already selected delegates to attend. It was Shay's Rebellion, that provided the urgency for the remaining states to select their delegates and participate in the upcoming event (Steward 17).

As time went by, friction began to develop between the northern states and the southern states over economic development. The northern states wanted to concentrate more on manufacturing and shipping. Southern states were concentrating on building an agrarian economy, based on large plantations and slavery. That's a double whammy. Debates and heated discussions probably occurred in Congress over where to spend money in economic development. And on top of that, slavery always was the big elephant in the room, although many preferred not to deal with it at the time.

- **Congress did not have the power to regulate foreign or domestic commerce.**

Trade was difficult between states. Each state had their own currency and often they charged taxes when bringing goods from one state to another. Think how difficult this would be today with so many trucks on the interstate highways. Every time they cross a state line, they would have to stop, pay a tax, and possibly exchange their currency at another stop. Interstate commerce would be crippled by such actions.

- **For the most part, only Congress had the power to conduct foreign relations.**

"No state, without the consent of the United States in Congress assembled, shall send any embassy to, or receive any embassy from, or enter into any conference, agreement, alliance, or treaty with any king, prince or state" (Articles of Confederation Transcript, Article VI).

Furthermore, the foundation was laid to prevent a noble class from ever developing in the United States.

"…nor shall any person holding any office of profit or trust under the United States, or any of them, accept of any present, emolument, office or title of any kind whatever from any king, prince, or foreign state; nor shall the United States in Congress assembled, or any of them, grant any title of nobility" (Transcription of Articles of Confederation, Article VI).

- Other European countries looked upon the new United States as a group of regional entities, very poor, and somewhat backward.

That image presented numerous problems for a young nation trying to deal with other more established nations.

- One last interesting article concerning Canada.

It appears our founding fathers had high hopes that Canada would join our new confederation.

"Canada acceding to this Confederation, and joining in the measures of the United States, shall be admitted into and entitled to all the advantages of this union; but no other colony shall be admitted into the same unless such admission be agreed by nine states" (Transcription of Articles of Confederation, Article XI).

This wish never materialized.

Much of the wording and characteristics in the *Articles of Confederation* resembled those found in a league, rather than a nation. Others proved to be such a challenge to governing that people began to question if our new government could provide our young country with the goods and services it needed. Our Founding Fathers, framers of the Constitution and the statesmen of the day began to realize the *Articles of Confederation* was inadequate to meet the challenges of the time. There was little to no sign of nationality and the movement toward nationality was greatly obstructed by the *Articles of Confederation* itself. Furthermore, representatives from the various states functioned like foreign diplomats. Resolutions and laws passed by the representatives in Congress, often proved to be inadequate. Without state ratification, nothing really happened. Thus, from 1783-1787, the civil powers of the United States tended strongly toward disintegration and ruin. The *Articles of Confederation* had become a government of shreds and patches. Those more thoughtful believed a new political system would have to be devised or all would be lost (Ridpath, 352-353).

On a side note, there were two important accomplishments during the period of the *Articles of Confederation*:

1. **Organization of the territory northwest of the Ohio River.**

   The campaign of George Rogers Clark in 1778-1779 had wrestled the territory northwest of the Ohio River from the British. This vast domain between the Allegheny and the Mississippi River was previously claimed by four states; Virginia, New York, Massachusetts, and Connecticut.

   A good example of the founding father's willingness to compromise, in the interest of unity, occurred when Virginia agreed for the good of the new country to cede the lands north of the Ohio River to the United States. Another was when Connecticut ceded claimed land to Pennsylvania in 1782. Over the next few years, other states would also cede lands to the new nation in the interest of growth and unity.

LAND CLAIMS OF THE STATES

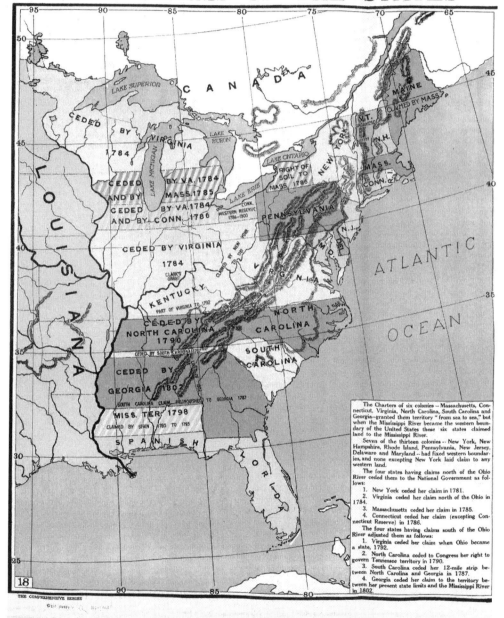

The Charters of six colonies -- Massachusetts, Connecticut, Virginia, North Carolina, South Carolina and Georgia--granted them territory "from sea to sea," but when the Mississippi River became the western boundary of the United States these six states claimed land to the Mississippi River.

Seven of the thirteen colonies -- New York, New Hampshire, Rhode Island, Pennsylvania, New Jersey, Delaware and Maryland -- had fixed western boundaries, and none excepting New York laid claim to any western land.

The four states having claims north of the Ohio River ceded them to the National Government as follows:

1. New York ceded her claim in 1781.
2. Virginia ceded her claim north of the Ohio in 1784.
3. Massachusetts ceded her claim in 1785.
4. Connecticut ceded her claim (excepting Connecticut Reserve) in 1786.

The four states having claims south of the Ohio River adjusted them as follows:

1. Virginia ceded her claim when Ohio became a state, 1792.
2. North Carolina ceded to Congress her right to govern Tennessee territory in 1790.
3. South Carolina ceded her 12-mile strip between North Carolina and Georgia in 1787.
4. Georgia ceded her claim to the territory between her present state limits and the Mississippi River in 1802.

Image from McLaughlin, Andrew Cunningham. State Claims to Western Lands 1783-1802.

TERRITORIAL FORMATION 1783–1812

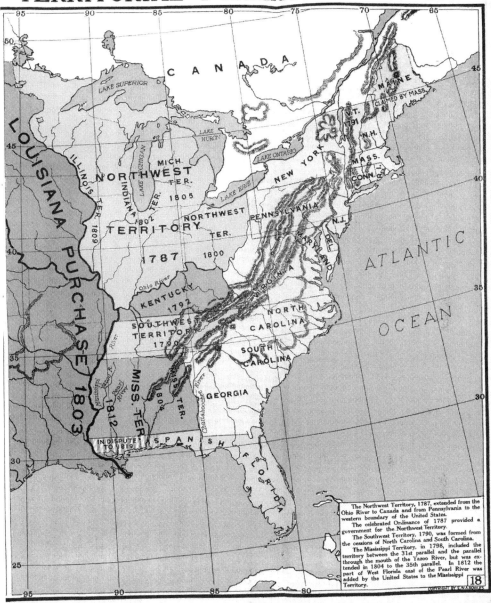

Image from McLaughlin, Andrew Cunningham. State Claims to Western Lands 1783-1802.

Now the question became how to manage this vast western region. Thomas Jefferson outlined his ideas in the form of an ordinance and presented it to Congress. On July 13, 1787, Congress adopted the ordinance for the governing of this vast new region. It stipulated:

A. Not fewer than three nor more than five states would be formed out of this vast western region.

B. Furthermore, when a new state was organized, it should be admitted to the union on terms of equality with the old thirteen states.

C. A liberal system of education should be assured to the inhabitants of the new commonwealths.

D. Slavery or involuntary servitude, except for the punishment of a crime, should be forever prohibited therein.

In time, five great states were organized and admitted to the United States under these provisions. They were the great states of Ohio, Indiana, Illinois, Michigan, and Wisconsin (Ridpath, 354-355).

2. **Adoption of the "Dollar."**

Following the war, England's monetary system was in use in the new United States. This meant people were paying for goods and services using guineas, pounds, shilling and pence. Thomas Jefferson proposed, and Congress agreed to "adopt the DOLLAR as our unit of account payment, and that its divisions and subdivisions shall be in the decimal ratio." This seemed to be a much easier and scientific system of money (Ridpath 355).

Despite these two important accomplishments, "it was clear to the statemen of that period that no effectual consolidation of the states had been accomplished by the *Articles of Confederation*" (Ridpath 359). In the west, the British still occupied some forts and Spain had closed the Mississippi River to Americans. They refused to allow Americans to traverse the Mississippi or to trade in New Orleans. This was devastating to westerns who relied on the Mississippi River for trade. In the northeast and the mid-Atlantic states, Britain still refused to trade with Americans, even in the West Indies and had not as yet sent a formal ambassador to America (Steward 21). Then there was the matter of the Barbary States in the Mediterranean seizing American ships and enslaving their crews (Stewart 10). In the south, Georgia had taken it upon themselves to wage war on the Creek Indians and Spain who controlled Florida was suspected of arming those native Americans. To make matters worse, the nation's credit was in ruin, the treasury was bankrupt, disorder was in the nation's finances, the characteristics of the *Articles of Confederation* now seemed crazy, and the government was without vital energy (Ridpath 359). Something had to be done.

Another movement of a more radical character would be necessary. One that would secure a real union of the United States of America and begin to resolve problems that became apparent during the years of the *Articles of Confederation*. Thus, a call went out to the thirteen states to send representatives to Philadelphia on the second Monday in May of 1787 to discuss reforming the *Articles of Confederation* (Ridpath 359).

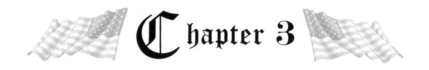

Chapter 3

1787
The Constitution of the United States

Fifty-five representatives showed up to discuss fine-tuning the *Articles of Confederation*. They were an interesting mix of people. Twenty-eight of them were lawyers. In addition, four were both lawyers and planters while eight were merchants, three were businessmen, one was an inventor (Benjamin Franklin), seven were planters, one was a politician, and three were doctors (Stewart ix-x). Furthermore, of the fifty-five who attended, only thirty-nine eventually signed the new document (Steward 282-284). Some left early because of business reasons, like Oliver Ellsworth from Connecticut and William Pierce from Georgia. Also, when the conversation turned from fine-tuning the *Articles of Confederation* to writing a new constitution, some didn't agree with this idea and went home. John Mercer, for example, from Maryland left in protest. Patrick Henry from Virginia and Luther Martin from Maryland did not sign because they believed it did not address the rights of states enough. Then there were those like Elbridge Gerry from Massachusetts and George Mason from Virginia who showed up but would not sign the document because initially there was no *Bill of Rights*. And finally, Edmund Randolf from Virginia did not sign the document because he believed it did not have enough checks and balances. Later, he changed his mind and worked to have it ratified in Virginia (The Delegates Who Didn't Sign the U.S. Constitution).

For most who did show up it soon became apparent they could not fine-tune the *Articles of Confederation*. Rather, they needed a new document that would produce a much stronger central federal government...one that could address the problems and challenges previously noted as well as protect our unalienable Rights. The trick was to strike a balance that would give the federal government the powers they needed to meet the challenges of needed goods and services while maintaining important human rights and civil liberties. At the same time, States were insisting upon retaining most of their powers so they could promulgate specific laws that did not infringe upon the central government.

Volumes have been written about the actual Constitutional Convention that convened on May 14, 1787 and lasted until 17, September 1787. It is not the intent of this publication to review the convention. Suffice it to say, the new *U.S. Constitution* and the *Bill of Rights* was ratified on December 15, 1791.

What incredible documents they turned out to be. Two of the greatest documents' mankind has ever produced. Embodied in these unique American documents are numerous enlightenment ideas, human rights and civil liberties that have made America a shining light on the planet. Today many people still seek to come to our shores to raise their families and enjoy the human rights and civil liberties these documents reaffirm. Below are just some of the ideas in those documents that have created in America, a unique political, social and economic culture for everyone.

Federalism

When the framers of the Constitution met in Philadelphia in May 14, 1787, they had basically two choices of government: A monarchy with a noble class to basically run the government. Or, they could choose a type of democratic government. They chose the latter.

They chose a democratic republic type of government because of the experiences they had as Englishmen, whereby the mother country often coerced citizens via a king and a noble class. Our founding fathers wanted none of that. By 1776, they had seen enough coercion, repression, and injustice to make the idea of having a government led by nobility with a king as the head of state, almost impossible. Instead they wanted a government whereby citizens would voluntarily consent to be governed. The *Articles of Confederation* put America on such a path.

However, by 1782, the *Articles of Confederation* were firmly in place and some could already see some of the difficulties mentioned earlier. In addition, the Treaty of Peace between the United States and Great Britain was being planned. It was to take place in September of 1783. Also, things on the frontier were in a holding pattern because, as noted previously, the British had refused to vacate several forts previously agreed to by both the British and the Americans. Because of this, the northern part of the army was encamped near Newburgh, New York while Washington's HQ (headquarters) was closed by at the Hasbrouck House in Newburgh (Newburgh Conspiracy).

Frustration with Congress was taking its toll in the army. Of major concern was whether or not they would be paid what was promised to them. There appeared to be a lack of faith in the new government on the part of some Continental Army officers. Most likely this was based on the difficulties the Continental Congress had during the war in raising needed supplies and in paying those serving in the Continental Army. On top of all this, in 1780 Congress voted to reduce by fifty percent, the pay for retired soldiers (Newburgh Conspiracy). And the individual States over the next few years were having trouble complying with the voluntary payments to replenish the amount of money needed to pay soldiers. It's no wonder that by 1782, even some of the soldiers began to doubt if they would ever receive their full compensation.

One in particular, Colonel Lewis Nicola, who was getting up in years being sixty-five years old and a veteran of the Revolutionary War, was extremely worried about receiving his pension money. His current assignment was commander of the invalid corps. As such he was in regular correspondence with General Washington about the status of the men. Thus, in one of his letters to the general, he indicated his pension concerns as well as his concerns for a Republican democratic government (Roos). Colonel Nicola wrote:

"...the same abilities which have lead us, through difficulties apparently insurmountable by human power, to victory and glory, those qualities that have merited and obtained the universal esteem and veneration of an army, would be most likely to conduct and direct us in the smoother paths of peace" (Roos). Furthermore, he wrote, "Some people have so connected the ideas of tyranny and monarchy as to find it very difficult to separate them, it may therefore be requisite to give the head of such a constitution as I propose, some title apparently more moderate, but if all other things were once adjusted I believe strong arguments might be produced for admitting the title of king, which I conceive would be attended with some material advantages" (Roos).

General Washington upon reading Nicola's letter, responded with the following correspondence.

"Be assured Sir, no occurrence in the course of the War, has given me more painful sensations than your information of there being such ideas existing in the Army as you have expressed, and I must view with abhorrence, and reprehend with severity. I am much at a loss to conceive what part of my conduct could have given encouragement to an address which to me seems big with the greatest mischiefs that can befall my Country. If I am not deceived in the knowledge of myself, you could not have found a person to whom your schemes are more disagreeable" (Roos).

Clearly Washington was dedicated to Congress by this response to Colonel Nicola. Yet, the concerns with Congress' inability to pay the army for services rendered was a growing concern. Officers and soldiers alike were beginning to think they may never be fully compensated for their services during the American Revolution. By 1783, these concerns were beginning to breed outright discontent to the point that some, anonymous as they were, planned to take outright action.

Such was the state of affairs on March 10, 1783, when Washington was made aware of a meeting that was planned to deal with grievances. Below is a copy of the paper which was being circulated among the army.

"A meeting of the general and field officers is requested at the public building, on Tuesday next, at 11 o'clock. A commissioned officer from each company is expected, and a delegate from the medical staff. The object of this convention is to consider the late letter from our representative in Philadelphia, and what measures (if any) should be adopted, to obtain that redress of grievances which they seem to have solicited in vain" (Journals of Congress 294-295).

As Washington was reviewing the above paper which was being circulated in the camp, he was made aware of a second anonymous paper that was also being circulated among the army in a clandestine manner. It read in part,

"Gentlemen,-A fellow soldier, whose interest and affections bind him strongly to you, whose past sufferings have been as great, and whose future fortune may be as desperate as yours-would beg leave to address you...

Like many of you, he loved private life and left it with regret. He left it, determined to retire from the field, with the necessity that called him to it, and not till then—not till the enemies of his country, the slaves of power, and the hirelings of injustice, were compelled to abandon their schemes, and acknowledge America as terrible in arms as she had been humble in remonstrance. With this objective in view, he has long shared in your toils and mingled in your dangers. He has felt the cold hand of poverty without a murmur, and has seen the insolence of wealth without a sigh. But, too much under the direction of his wishes, and sometimes weak enough to mistake desire for opinion, he has till lately—very lately—believed in the justice of his country. He hoped that, as the clouds of adversity scattered, and as the sunshine of peace and better fortune broke in upon us, the coldness and severity of government would relax, and that more than justice, that gratitude would blaze forth upon those hands, which had upheld her, in the darkest stages of her passage, from impending servitude to acknowledged independence...

After a pursuit of seven long years, the object for which we set out is at length brought within our reach. Yes, my friends, that suffering courage of yours was active once—it has conducted the United States of America through a doubtful and bloody war. It has placed her in the chair of independency, and peace returns again to bless—whom? A country willing to redress your wrongs, cherish your worth and reward your services, a country courting your return to private life, with tears of gratitude and smiles of admiration, longing to divide with you that independency which your gallantry has given, and those riches which your wounds have preserved? Is this the case? Or is it rather a country that tramples upon your rights, disdains your cries and insults your distresses? Have you not, more than once, suggested your wishes, and made known your wants to Congress? Wants and wishes which gratitude and policy should have anticipated, rather than evaded... How have you been answered? Let the letter which you are called to consider tomorrow make reply" (Journals of Congress 295-296).

In an effort to prevent any dangerous resolutions from occurring, Washington immediately moved to cancel the planned meeting for March 11, 1783. He called for a brief four-day period for everyone to calm down. He then scheduled a general meeting for all officers to be held on Saturday March 15, 1783. As he later recalled in a report to Congress, Washington issued the following order.

"General Orders—Headquarters, Newburgh, Tuesday March 11, 1783.

The Commander in Chief, having heard that a general meeting of the officers of the army was proposed to be held this day at the new building, in an anonymous paper which was circulated yesterday by some unknown person, conceived, although he is fully persuaded that the good sense of the officers would induce them to pay very little attention to such an irregular invitation, his duty, as well as the reputation and true interest of the army, requires his disapprobation of such disorderly proceedings. At the same time he requests the general and field-officers with one officer from each company, and a proper representation from the staff of the army, will assemble at 12 o'clock on Saturday next, at the new building, to hear the report of the committee of the army to Congress. After mature deliberation, they will devise what further measures ought to be adopted as most rational and best calculated to attain the just and important object in view. The senior officer in rank, present, will be pleased to preside, and report the result of the deliberations to the Commander in Chief" (Journals of Congress 297-298).

To show the gravity of the situation, yet another anonymous paper emerged as everyone waited for the Saturday next meeting. This paper suggested that Washington's silence thus far was an invitation to meet and address the grievances.

"...Till now the Commander in Chief has regarded the steps you have taken for redress, with good wishes alone. His ostensible silence has authorized your meetings, and his private opinion has sanctified your claims..." (Journals of Congress 299).

Nevertheless, calmer heads did prevail, and the officers waited until the planned meeting on Saturday March 15, at the new building in Newburgh, NY. Some thought Washington was not planning on attending the meeting because he had asked the senior officer in rank present to preside and report the results to him at a later date. However, when the time came, Washington did make a surprise visit. Upon entering the meeting, General Washington was immediately given the floor to speak. Here are excerpts from his speech which was written in a report to Congress.

"Gentlemen, -By an anonymous summons, an attempt has been made to convene you together. How inconsistent with the rules of propriety, how unmilitary and how subversive of all order and discipline, let the good sense of the army decide.

In the moment of this summons, another anonymous production was sent into circulation, addressed more to the feelings and passions than to the reason and judgment of the army...

Thus much, gentlemen, I have thought it incumbent on me to observe to you, to show upon what principles I opposed the irregular and hasty meeting which was proposed to have been held on Tuesday last, and not because I wanted a disposition to give you every opportunity, consistent with your own honor, and the dignity of the army, to make known your grievances...

If my conduct heretofore has not evinced to you that I have been a faithful friend to the army, my declaration of it at this time would be equally unavailing and improper. But as I am among the first who embarked in the cause of our common country; as I have never left your side one moment, but when called from you on public duty; as I have been the constant companion and witness of your distresses, and not among the last to feel and acknowledge your merits; as I have ever considered my own military reputation as inseparably connected with that of the army; as my heart has ever expanded with joy, when I have heard its praises, and my indignation has arisen when the mouth of detraction has been opened against it, it can scarcely be supposed, at this late stage of the war, that I am indifferent to its interests. But how are they to be promoted? The way is plain, says the anonymous addresser. 'If war continues, remove into the unsettled country; there establish yourselves and leave an ungrateful country to defend itself.' – But who are they to defend? Our wives, our children, our farms and other property which we leave behind us? Or, in this state of hostile separation, are we to take the two first (the latter cannot be removed) to perish in a wilderness with hunger, cold and nakedness? 'If peace takes place, never sheath your swords,' says he 'until you have Obtained full and ample justice.' This dreadful alternative of either deserting our country in the extremest hour of her distress, or turning our arms against it, which is the apparent object, unless Congress can be compelled into instant compliance, has something so shocking in it, that humanity revolts at the idea. My God! What can this writer have in view, by recommending such measures? Can he be a friend to the army? Can he be a friend to this country? Rather is he not an insidious foe? Some emissary, perhaps from New York, plotting the ruin of both, by sowing the seeds of discord and separation between the civil and military powers of the continent...?

With respect to the advice given by the author...I

spurn it, as every man who regards that liberty and reveres that justice for which we contend...I cannot, in justice to my own belief, and what I have great reason to conceive is the intention of Congress, conclude this address, without giving it as my decided opinion, that honorable body entertain exalted sentiments of the services of the army, and from a full conviction of its merits and sufferings, will do it complete justice: That their endeavors to discover and establish funds for this purpose have been unwearied, and will not cease till they have succeeded, I have not a doubt.

But like all other large bodies, where there is a variety of different interests to reconcile, their determinations are slow. Why then should we distrust them, and, in consequence of that distrust, adopt measures which may cast a shade over that glory which has been so justly acquired, and tarnish the reputation of an army which is celebrated through all Europe for its fortitude and patriotism? And for what is this done? To bring the object we seek nearer? No, most certainly, in my opinion, it will cast it at a greater distance...

I feel for an army I have so long had the honor to command, will oblige me to declare, in this public and solemn manner, that in the attainment of complet justice for all your toils and dangers, and in the gratification of every wish so far as may be done consistently with the great duty I owe my country, and those powers we are bound to respect, you may freely command my services to the utmost extent of my abilities.

While I give you these assurances, and pledge myself in the most unequivocal manner, to exert whatever ability, I am possessed of in your favor, let me entreat you, gentlemen, on your part, not to take any measures, which, viewed in the calm light of reason will lessen the dignity, and sully the glory you have hitherto maintained. Let me request you to rely on the plighted faith of your country, and place a full confidence in the purity of the intentions of Congress..." (Journals of Congress 306-309).

In closing, General Washington pulled a letter of support from Congressman Joseph Jones from Virginia from his coat pocket. He began to read it to his officers. However, his eyesight wasn't what it used to be so reading it was difficult. After the first paragraph he reached for a pair of eyeglasses, also in his coat pocket and said,

"Gentlemen, you must pardon me, for I have not only grown gray but almost blind in the service to my country (Newburgh Conspiracy)." Tears began to flow from some of his officers. When he finished reading the letter, General Washington left the room (Newburgh Conspiracy).

His officers then responded by drafting a resolution of unanimous thanks...

"His Excellency having withdrawn, on motion by General Knox, seconded by General Putnam,
Resolved, That the unanimous thanks of the officers of the army be presented to his Excellency the Commander in Chief, for his excellent address, and the communication he has been pleased to make to them; and that he be assured that the officers reciprocate his affectionate expressions, with the greatest sincerity of which the human heart is capable."

Furthermore, it was also resolved unanimously,

"...the officers of the American army engaged in the service of their country from the purest love and attachment to the rights and liberties of human nature, which motives still exist in the highest degree; and that no circumstances of distress or danger shall induce a conduct that may tend to sully the reputation and glory which they have acquired, at the price of their blood and eight years' faithful services. Also,

That the army continue to have an unshaken confidence in the justice of Congress and their country, and are fully convinced that the representatives of America will not disband or disperse the army until their accounts are liquidated, the balances accurately ascertained, and adequate funds established for payment, and in this arrangement, the officers expect that the half-pay, or a commutation of it, should be efficaciously comprehended..." (Journals of Congress 309-310).

These two events, the letter from Colonel Nicola and the Newburgh Conspiracy, as it has since been labeled, made the likelihood of a future monarchy in America or a military takeover of the government by the army, very unlikely. However, they did highlight major concerns with how Congress was functioning and its ability to resolve, at least some of the challenges it faced. By 1786, not only Washington but a number of the founding fathers were convinced that changes had to be made to the *Articles of Confederation* if the United States was to survive as a new nation. Washington and many of the founding fathers and statesmen of the day became involved in a national movement for governmental reform. They continued to push for a convention to reform the *Articles of Confederation*. Finally, the states agreed to a conference to be held in Philadelphia in the spring of 1787. And when the time came, in 1787, to travel to Philadelphia, Washington, despite being sick that winter, made sure he was one of the four delegates chosen from Virginia to attend the conference. There was no way Washington was going to miss this opportunity to reform the government. No doubt because of his personal experiences in the army, he felt a sense of urgency to this task. As he noted to Henry Know in a letter on February 3, 1787, "like a house on fire, whilst the most regular form of extinguishing it is contended for, the building is reduced to ashes" (To Henry Knox, Mount Vernon, February 3, 1787). Meaning if the government wasn't fixed soon, it was going to collapse.

When Washington arrived in Philadelphia in May of 1787, along with the other delegates from most states, they soon realized it would be difficult to fix the *Articles of Confederation*. What they needed was a different type of government that could fix the current problems and challenges and at the same time be acceptable to the States. Discussions soon turned to Federalism.

Federalism is a type of democratic government that enables people to give their consent to be governed through elected representatives. Furthermore, any group of citizens can be known as a commonwealth, for example, the Commonwealth of Pennsylvania. These groups, commonwealths/states, agree to become a country/republic without having a monarch. They also agree the central government of this republic will be the supreme power. Representatives chosen by the people through democracy/voting, will have the power to make laws and govern the country. Ancient Rome had such a republic before it was usurped by strong men and later ruled by emperors.

This unique form of government designed by the framers of the Constitution, was in essence, an evolution of the *Articles of Confederation*. It became known as "**Dual Federalism**" because the States ended up retaining those powers not specifically spelled out in the Constitution. However, those powers specifically noted in the Constitution for the federal government became supreme.

Such an arrangement/compromise was necessary because under the *Articles of Confederation*, each colony became a state in and of itself. Even the British recognized this when they signed the *Treaty of Peace* on September 3. Under Article I, it read, "His Britannic Majesty acknowledges the said United States, viz New Hampshire, (all thirteen colonies were then listed)...to be free sovereign and independent States." Furthermore, under Article V, "Persons shall have free Liberty to go to any Part or Parts of any of the thirteen United States and therein to remain twelve months Unmolested" (Definitive Treaty of Peace). This concept under the *Articles of Confederation* became a problem because there was no way the states were going to give up all their power to govern. Each State was independent and sovereign in its decisions. Representatives sent to Congress by the States, not the people, functioned like diplomats, unable to pass real binding legislation. This meant that legislation passed would have to be approved later by the States. As time went by, this proved almost impossible for all thirteen states to comply with *Articles of Confederation* legislation. As a result, funds raised were often insufficient to meet the challenges of national issues like paying debts or paying soldiers pensions or even their pay, building bridges or developing western lands. Some States gave money, others delayed or bulked at the payments requested by Congress. Something had to be done if we were truly going to build a new nation.

Imagine going to the Constitutional Convention in the summer of 1787 and trying to not only compromise on details but reach a balance of power between a stronger federal government and the individual States. Men such as James Madison, Dickenson, and General C.C. Pinckney were all for a strong central government, so long as the States would retain considerable power (Berger 53). Thus, it came to pass through much discussion and compromise, the framers reached a balance of power for both the Federal Government and the individual State Governments.

The basis of power for the Federal Government rests in the *Supremacy Clause*. Article VI, second paragraph reads,

> "This Constitution, and the Laws of the United States which shall be made in Pursuance thereof; and all Treaties made, or which shall be made, under the Authority of the United States, shall be the supreme Law of the land; and the Judges in every State shall be bound thereby, any Thing in the Constitution or Laws of any State to the Contrary notwithstanding" (The Constitution of the United States: A Transcription).

In other words, laws passed by the Federal Government take precedent over any State Laws.

Furthermore, the opening paragraph prior to Article I, is often referred to, which broadens the Federal Government's powers. It reads,

> "We the People of the United States, in Order to form a more perfect Union, establish Justice, ensure domestic Tranquility, provide for the common defense, promote the general welfare, and secure the Blessings of Liberty to ourselves and our Posterity, do ordain and establish this Constitution for the United States of America" (The Constitution of the United States: A Transcription).

These phrases allowed the new Federal Republic to pass legislation which all States had to abide by. Thus, the framers were able to correct the inefficiencies of the *Articles of Confederation* and build a new nation. They were able to establish one system of currency, one system for commerce, one military to protect the nation, one judicial system for judging federal laws and so on and so on.

Any other powers, not described in the Constitution, were reserved for the States. For example, nowhere in the Constitution will you find the word education. It was left up to each individual State to educate their youth as they see fit. Of course, today things are somewhat more complicated. Scholars and politicians continually debate where the line for power is drawn.

In addition, there are powers today that both the Federal Government and individual States both have. These types of powers are called "**Concurrent Powers**." Taxes are a good example of this. The Federal Government taxes individual's incomes while the states, if they choose, can also tax an individual's income. There is also a federal gasoline tax and state gasoline taxes which help with the maintenance of roads. In addition, states can organize school districts as they see fit and determine curriculum. States can also run and manage both local and state elections. Some state's elections are held on one day. In other states, there is early voting and internet voting. Each state also has a constitution and a legislature. Some are patterned after the federal government with a House and a Senate. In Nebraska there is a non-partisan unicameral legislature which means there is only one house with elected representatives (Senators) to manage the laws of the state of Nebraska. Also, states have the ability like the federal government to borrow money and create state banks. Lastly, states have the ability to enforce their laws with local and state police forces.

The bottom line is the founding fathers and statesmen who designed the Constitution, developed an incredible system of government, with an ability to make changes for future generations. It is a system that has enabled the States to continue to have state and local power within the framework of a strong central federal government. Below are some additional concepts and details that were included in the *United States Constitution*. They are all part of what makes the American political, social and economic system unique, even to this day.

Checks & Balances

Charles-Louis de Secondat, Baron de Montesquieu
(1689-1755)

One of the most influential philosophers and authors admired by our founding fathers was Charles-Louis de Secondat, Baron de Montesquieu. In his book, *Spirit of the Laws*, published in 1748, he argued for a government with a system of checks and balances.

Montesquieu was a Frenchman. His occupation was a judge and as such, he was well aware of the abuses of power by the French monarchs. He also was aware of the many grievances the French people had against their government and the reforms they desired. All that was stopping reform was the absolute power held by the king.

It was not until after Montesquieu's death in 1788 that Louis XVI was forced to think about reform. What a shame for Louis XVI and France that he did not buy into the political ideas of Charles-Louis de Secondat, Baron de Montesquieu. He might have survived and become a constitutional monarch, like the government that developed in England. Sadly, Louis XVI did not believe in Montesquieu's ideas on government. He was eventually executed for crimes against France.

The founding fathers on the other hand did believe in Baron de Montesquieu's ideas. When the delegates from the thirteen States met in Philadelphia, PA in 1787, to consider fine-tuning the *Articles of Confederation* or drafting a new constitution, it was Montesquieu's ideas that became central to the new document that would lay the groundwork for a new government. Here are just a few of those ideas which found their way into the U.S. Constitution.

Equal Divisions of Power In A Government

This means there should be several equal branches of power in a government. The intent of this was to prevent the concentration of power in any one of the branches, especially in the executive branch. Montesquieu witnessed what too much power in the hands of a king could do to a society. Most likely it was also hoped equal divisions of power in government would minimize corruption. Because of Montesquieu, our founding fathers chose a government with three equal branches.

- **Executive Branch** (Headed by the President)
- **A Bi-cameral Legislature** (Congress; composed of a Senate and a House of Representatives)
- **A Judicial Branch** (Composed of smaller courts that led to a Supreme Court)

The Executive Branch

Think of the President as a CEO with multiple subsidiary companies which must be managed day by day. However, it gets more complicated for a President. In addition to following the laws of the land, a President has other regulations and restrictions that a true CEO is not bound by. The President of the United States is charged with the responsibilities of not only following the laws and governmental regulations, he or she is also charged with the responsibility of implementing and enforcing them as well. In addition, the President serves as head of the government for diplomatic purposes and from time to time travels to important international conferences. Also, the President is the Commander in Chief of the armed services. In the event of a war, it is the President who is responsible for managing the war with the U.S. armed forces.

Today, the Executive Branch is huge. According to the White House, there are over four million people currently working in the Executive Branch (Our Government The Executive Branch). That number may be approaching three million today. This mass of people, often referred to as the federal bureaucracy, is further broken down into various general areas, each managed by a person in the President's cabinet. Below are the current cabinet positions:

- Vice-President
- Agriculture
- Commerce
- Defense
- Education
- Energy
- Health & Human Services
- Homeland Security
- Housing & Urban Development

- Interior
- Labor
- State Department
- Transportation
- Treasury
- Veterans Affairs
- Attorney General

Our Government
The Executive Branch

The President has other miscellaneous responsibilities. They include managing public relations, correspondence, social and visits by foreign dignitaries as well as managing the White House housekeeping staff. Imagine the power the President has with control over this civilian government work force and the military. It is no wonder the founding fathers adopted the Baron's ideas of checks and balances. They did not want the President in any way to become or function like a king of old or in today's world, to become a dictator.

The Legislative Branch

It is the job of Congress to formulate and pass laws, not a monarch or a president or a prime minister. Currently, there are 435 members in the House of Representatives and 100 members in the Senate, two from each state directly elected by the voting population in that state. If there is a tie in the Senate, the Vice-President casts the deciding vote.

In order for legislation to become a law of the land, it needs to be passed by both the House of Representatives and the Senate by a simple majority. However, there are times when a two-thirds vote is required for the law to pass. These situations are spelled out by law and the constitution. After that, it goes to the President to sign or to veto. If the President signs the bill/legislation, it becomes law. If the President veto's the bill/legislation, then the House and Senate must re-pass the bill by a two-thirds majority for it to become law. This is the check and balance on the Legislative Branch.

The Judiciary Branch, Article III

Section 1, "The judicial Power of the United States, shall be vested in one supreme Court, and in such inferior

Courts as the Congress may from time to time ordain and establish" (The Constitution of the United States: A Transcription).

Today there is one Supreme Court composed of nine judges who, if appointed and ratified by the Senate, serve for life or as long as they choose. One of the judges is chosen to be the Chief Justice. Below the Supreme Court are thirteen appellate courts also known as U.S. Courts of Appeal. Below the appellate courts are ninety-four federal district courts organized into twelve regional circuits each of which has its own court of appeals. There is one more regional court known as the 13th court or Court of Appeals for the Federal Circuit located in Washington, D.C. (Judicial Branch).

The primary purpose of these courts is to interpret laws passed by the legislature and signed by the President. They are the check and balance for both the legislature and the President. Cases are presented to the courts and often work their way up to the Supreme Court. Once at the Supreme Court, the nine justices take months to review the case and then report their findings. Five of the nine judges or more are needed for a decision to become binding. Also, one of the judges who voted with the majority is selected to write a review of the case and report that to the public.

Each branch can be checked in its exercise of power by other branches

As noted earlier, if the President veto's a bill/legislation, it means that cannot go into effect until both the House of Representatives and the Senate re-pass the bill/legislation by a two-thirds majority. The veto power by the President is the check and balance on the legislature. That's the check and balance the President has over Congress. The check and balance on the President is Congress' ability to repass a law by a two-thirds majority vote that the President vetoed. If such an event takes place, the bill/legislation becomes law despite the presidential veto.

Another check and balance on both presidential power and Congress is the Supreme Court's ability to review an executive order or a direct order by the president or a law passed by Congress and signed by the president, to declare it unconstitutional. If such an event takes place, the executive order or the direct order or the law immediately becomes null and void.

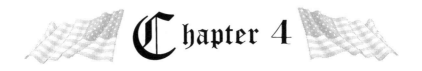

Chapter 4

1791
Important Human and Civil Rights in The United States Bill of Rights and ensuing Amendments

After the Constitution was written, many founding fathers feared it might not be ratified. They believed several important human rights were not spelled out clearly enough in the constitution. Therefore, a "Bill of Rights" was needed and was written and presented along with the constitution for the states to ratify. Rhode Island was the last state to ratify the United States Constitution, including the *Bill of Rights*, thus making it the law of the land in 1791.

Below are a few of the more important human and civil rights that were so cherished by our founding fathers, that they were included in the *United States Bill of Rights*.

Religious Freedom/Toleration and Separation of Church & State

Bill of Rights, Amendment I

"Congress shall make no laws respecting an establishment of religion"
(The Bill of Rights: A Transcription).

The idea of religious freedom came from numerous philosophes in Europe. John Locke, argued for religious freedom in his "Letter Concerning Toleration." He established a powerful foundation for not only religious liberty but religious toleration as well. In addition, he argued for separation of church and state. No doubt the Wars of Religion played a major role in the development of his ideas. Before, during his lifetime and thereafter, over a million people throughout Europe lost their life trying to defend their right to worship whatever religion they chose.

Cases in point included the Spanish Armada which sailed for England in 1588 with the purpose of restoring Catholicism in England. It was defeated when a terrible storm off the Irish coast sank many ships and subsequent naval battles led by famous English captains like Sir Francis Drake occurred offshore when the remaining ships finally arrived off the coast of England.

Then there was the struggle of the protestant Huguenots for religious freedom in France. Or, the struggle of the people in the Spanish Netherlands and the Dutch Republic (Belgium and Holland today) against Spain.

Image from the Library of Congress

And of course, they fought in Germany (remnants of the old Holy Roman Empire) over whether those lands would be Lutheran or Catholic.

François-Marie Arouet
(Voltaire)
(1694-1778)

Voltaire (his real name was François-Marie Arouet) was another great French philosopher who advocated religious freedom and toleration. During his travels in England, he praised the virtues of the English, especially their religious liberty. Furthermore, he criticized the lack of religious liberty in France. This did not sit well with the king of France. In fact, upon his return home French king Louis XVI had him imprisoned for a brief time simply for speaking his mind. Voltaire also wrote Candide which was a satire against war and religious persecution. In time, Voltaire became a major voice throughout Europe attacking religious persecution and advocating religious toleration.

Another philosopher, Gotthold Lessing was a German philosopher, playwright and critic, who championed religious toleration. In his book, *Nathan the Wise*, he advocated for religious toleration of not only different Christian sects, but also between different religions like Islam and Judaism (Gotthold Ephraim Lessing).

In addition to Lessing, Moses Mendelssohn was a German Jewish philosopher known as the "Jewish Socrates." He too argued for religious toleration. He did not believe any religions have a right to force their beliefs on others. He also advocated for allowing Jews to practice their religion freely (Plen).

We could go on and on but by now you probably understand our founding fathers probably read most of the philosopher literature on religion toleration and separation of church and state. Truly, they believed whole heartedly in these two concepts. The last thing they wanted in America was political or violent conflict as a result of religion. They also did not want any one religious sect or group to force their beliefs on another person or sect/group or individual.

This brings us to a modern case in point about forcing religious beliefs on others. It also highlights how extremely important this concept of separation of church and state is, even today in America.

Sometimes the subject of prayer in schools comes up in discussions. People often argue how things were better in the late 1950s and early 60s when the day began in most schools with a Christian prayer. At that time, all students were required to stand for a morning prayer, or at least they were in many schools.

It might surprise some people to know Christian students today, in many schools, are still allowed to pray either before or after school. Generally, a room is made available for them so they can meet and pray together. The same is true for any Muslim students or Jewish students who may wish to pray.

What is not acceptable is to force all students to pray a specific religious prayer. Perhaps those people who argue for beginning the school day in home room with a Christian prayer haven't thought much about students of other religious faiths which are in homeroom. What if the tables were turned around so that students would begin the day with a non-Christian prayer? For example, tomorrow the day will begin with a Muslim prayer in homeroom and all Christian students are asked to stand for the prayer. Then, on Wednesday the day will begin with a Jewish prayer and Thursday a Hindu prayer. One must wonder if Christian students and parents would accept such an arrangement?

Think of this little scenario as a case study in separation of church and state. Since schools are considered in the public sector (unless it is a specific religious school like a Catholic school), it would be unacceptable to force any students to pray a specific religious prayer other than a prayer of their religion. So, the best option is to allow students of a specific religion, prior to or after school to pray in a separate room.

Voila, everyone is happy and the enlightenment ideas of toleration and separation of church and state are maintained. Think about it! Our founding fathers were wise beyond their years. They perhaps foresaw this scenario over two hundred years ago and provided a governmental system that would allow everyone to express their religious beliefs without forcing any one group's religious beliefs on everyone. Sounds like a perfect solution in the twenty-first century to the question of prayer in public schools.

One final note...The Supreme Court needs to decide on universal standards for religion in American businesses. By this we mean if a Christian baker can be fined for refusing to bake a cake for a gay couple's wedding, then the same should hold true for a Muslim flight attendant who refuses to serve alcohol to a customer on a plane trip. Instead of terminating the flight attendant, a fine should have been issued to the flight attendant as it was in the case of the baker. Or, a company should not hire people with religious beliefs who are in opposition to a company's business. No matter what, it must be fair for everyone.

Freedom of Speech

Bill of Rights, Amendment I, ratified 15 December 1791

> "Congress shall make no law...prohibiting the free exercise thereof; or abridging...freedom of speech" (The Bill of Rights: A Transcription).

We see this Enlightenment idea also in the *Declaration of the Rights of Man and of the Citizen*, (a French document written during the French Revolution in 1789 before the *Bill of Rights* in 1791). In articles #10-11. "No one should be disturbed on account of his opinions, even religious, provided their manifestation does not upset the public order established by law…The free communication of ideas and opinions is one of the most precious of the rights of man; every citizen can then freely speak, write, and print, subject to responsibility for the abuse of this freedom in the cases as determined by law" (Anderson 58-60).

What did the French and Founding Fathers mean by this? Well, on the one hand they say you are free to say anything. Yet, you are not free to say anything, especially if there is a law against it.

In America, we have freedom of speech. But we also have laws which prohibit saying certain things. For example, there are laws on the books prohibiting anyone from screaming "Fire" in a theatre or public assembly. The idea behind this is that screaming "Fire," when there isn't a fire in the building could result in bodily injury or even death as a result of people frantically trying to exit the building. If you yell "Fire," as a joke or in trying to create a fake emergency to watch how people react, and even one person gets injured exiting the building, you will be held accountable. Which means, if you are found to be guilty in a court of law of such an irresponsible act, you could have to pay medical bills for those injured or even go to jail.

Another example of freedom of speech that can be hurtful and or harmful to others concerns students in school. Teachers are sometimes asked why students are taught about the *First Amendment to The United States Constitution* and then denied freedom of speech in school. The answer lies in concerns for the welfare of others.

Think of the discomfort caused when people feel free to say hateful words or display hateful words on a t-shirt, automobile, or anything else that would be emotionally hurtful to other persons. For example, the hurtful impact of a student wearing a t-shirt to school emblazoned with words expressing hate against a group. What a demeaning effect this would have on students who may have family history, even negative personal history, from past intolerant experiences based on ethnicity or culture. There is learned history about past human atrocities, such as: slavery; the Klu Klux Klan and white supremacy; American Indians; Black Panthers and civil rights; wars, such as the Civil War; the bombing of Pearl Harbor and the subsequent internment of Japanese Americans in camps; World War II and the Nazi death camps/The Holocaust; the Vietnam War; and todays treatment of immigrants seeking asylum at the borders. This historical knowledge provides awareness of the harshness on groups of people during these times. Freedom of speech, which is a right of all living in America, should have social, humane, and legal responsibility. Freedom of speech does not give anyone the right to cause others to relive uncomfortable times in history, nor live in fear. All Americans should feel confident knowing they can work, worship, learn, and be where hatred is not and will not be tolerated in word or deed. People should feel protected as human beings, knowing there will be social, legal, or judicial consequences taken against those who perpetuate hatred in any form.

Having freedom of speech is awesome. However, with it comes social and legal responsibilities that everyone should observe.

Freedom of the Press

Bill of Rights, Amendment I, ratified December 15, 1791

> "Congress shall make no law...prohibiting the free exercise thereof; or abridging...the freedom of the press (The Bill of Rights: A Transcription).

Perhaps the greatest invention of the post medieval world was the printing press. It was invented by a German goldsmith named Johannes Gutenberg sometime around 1445 A.D. Little did Gutenberg know then how this one invention would change the world.

Within the next three and a half centuries, more and more people learned to read because books and publications were being produced faster than ever. This explosion of publications and people reading more and more about all types of things, expanded their knowledge of the world greatly. In time, even an encyclopedia was published. Denis Diderot & Jean Rond d' Alembert, with the help of many others, published an encyclopedia in 1772. This work encompassed enlightenment ideas as well as scientific discoveries, theories, famous people and much more. The Encyclopedia was an attempt to make the "science of the day" available to people and to secularize learning. Its effect was to sometimes undermine old religious beliefs about the world (Denis Diderot).

The result of all this was people began to question what they were often told by the church and by the government. People, like the philosophes, searched for ways to make government and society better for all classes.

At the same time, society saw the emergence of coffee houses which served as centers for discussions. The first coffee house in London opened in "1652 on St. Michael's Ally, off Cornhill. It was run by Pasqua Rosee, a valet to businessman Daniel Edwards, an importer of goods from Turkey. News often was discussed at this coffee house. And, eventually a newsletter was produced and disseminated." (London's Original and All-Inspiring Coffee House).

In time, many coffee houses sprang up, each with their own clientele. For example, Man's coffee house was frequented by "bribe-lovers, Puritan-haters, French agents and mysterious messengers" (The Coffee Houses London).

In the Puritan's Coffee House politics were usually discussed. Frequent visitors talked of days gone by when Cromwell was in charge and dreamed of replacing King Charles II. At the Widow's Café, apprentices came to talk of unions and freemasonry. Financial matters, insurance and trade were generally the topics of conversation at Johnathan's, Lloyds and the Jamaica. Doctors frequented Garraway's and Child's where medicine was discussed. And, at The Grecian, philosophers and scholars often discussed the most recent events at the Royal Society (The Coffee Houses of London).

Eventually, even pubs became places to discuss ideas. And, in France, England and other countries, salons were filled with reform minded nobles.

Thus, more and more people were able to expand their knowledge of the world by either discussing the latest news at coffee houses, pubs or salons and by reading published newsletters.

As time went by, more and more people wanted the ability to discuss news and emerging scientific discoveries. This meant not only free speech but the ability to write, print, and to read news. Governments often felt threatened by all this dissemination of knowledge and tried to prevent it. The previous story of Voltaire's imprisonment upon his return to France from England for writing about England's toleration of religion, is a perfect example of freedom of the press clashing with a government's ability to try and control public opinion.

Fortunately for Americans, our founding fathers felt the positives outweighed the negatives and included freedom of the press in the *Bill of Rights*. Today we enjoy this right, despite its ability to present challenges at time. Case in point, would be someone wearing a printed shirt with a design of a Confederate battle flag on it. In many schools, this student would be told to go home and change the shirt.

School administrators often try and explain to a student why wearing such a shirt can be emotionally harmful and hurtful to other students. Then there is a question of whether the student wearing the shirt understands what it may mean to others. A response often heard is "it means personal freedom."

The other side of the coin concerns others. Almost a million Americans lost their life fighting to free slaves. This institutional scourge, by 1860, had become incompatible with *The Declaration of Independence* as well as the Constitution of the United States. Black people under slavery were subject to whippings, rape, torture, and even death by their masters. In addition, it was almost impossible to obtain their freedom, like with the old indentured servant program in the colonies during the early 1700s. In fact, if a slave tried to run away and was caught, they could be maimed, tortured or even hung. Also, sometimes families were split apart when a master decided to sell a parent or their children to someone else. In short, it was a barbaric, horrendous, evil institution that needed to be eliminated from American society. After all, England had banned slavery in 1833. It took effect on August 28, 1834.

Admittedly, people have every right today to fly a confederate flag on their truck or at their property. They do not have the right to display that image in some public places like government facilities. To fly a confederate flag at a state capital would be very hurtful to most African Americans and others. It stands for hate and has no place in a public setting. Also, it would be a dishonor to those nearly one million Americans who died fighting to eliminate slavery, settle the question of unfettered states' rights, and to save the Union. There is another challenge today brought about by freedom of the press. The proliferation of propaganda via social media.

In fact, it may be even more difficult today to discover the truth than it was in 1934. Why is this? Because often the truth lies somewhere between the spinning lens of radical polarization by social media and foreign powers. People get so confused today about what the truth is, they simply say "Oh, that's fake news." By these very words, they are giving validity to the power of propaganda.

For years this phrase has been used by both conservatives and liberals in America. Lately, "fake news" was used to soften the potential blow that might be made by the special prosecutor investigating Russian interference during the 2016 elections. The report by the special prosecutor wasn't even released for over two years. Yet, when it finally was released, many people heralded it as "fake news" before they even read it! That's really dangerous for all Americans.

Another example concerns President Obama's birth certificate. There is factual evidence he was born in Hawaii. Thus, he is an American citizen, despite the many emails sent through social media proclaiming President Obama was born in Kenya. If those emails had been true, it would have meant he was not eligible to run for the Presidency. Perhaps, those who believed this never thought through this scenario. So, let's think about this.

His mother went to Kenya to have her baby. When he was born, she called someone in Hawaii and got them to falsify the records at the hospital to make it look like he had been born in Hawaii. Then, someone on her behalf, got the newspaper to publish his birth in Hawaii. Lastly, she paid someone on the inside at the Hawaii records department to also falsify his birth records to show he was born in the United States in Hawaii. All of this accomplished so that years later, he could run for the Presidency of the United States.

Who in their right mind would believe such nonsense? It simply is too hard to believe. Yet, the power of propaganda tells us that many people still believe this. In a CBS poll taken in April of 2011, a quarter of all Americans believed President Obama was not born in the United States (Condon). By 2017, according to a YouGov poll, fifty-one percent of Republicans still believed President Obama was born in Kenya (Glum). In fact, we can find people in 2019 who still believe President Obama was born in Kenya.

That's the power of propaganda at work in America. People have heard this over and over for years. After a while, some begin to believe it is true.

This is reminiscent of Adolf Hitler in Germany during the 1930s when the Nazi party was campaigning to win the most seats in the Reichstag. Joseph Goebbels (a Nazi party member and later to become Minister of Propaganda) asked Hitler if it was ethical to lie to the German people in their political news/advertisements. Hitler looked at Goebbels with a stern face and said, "it's not truth that matters, but victory" (Adolf Hitler Quotes). He also said, "if you tell a big enough lie and tell it frequently enough, it will be believed" (Fifty Famous Quotes by Hitler).

People in both Italy and Germany, during the fascist regimes of Mussolini and Hitler, were led down a deep, dark troubling path because they never were told the truth. In 1932, when the Nazi party became the dominant party in the Reichstag and later, the *Reichstag Fire Decree* went into effect, Germans had little opportunity to listen to an opposing side of a debate. The government controlled the press, the radio, everything. Consequently, everything you read or heard was for the most part, propaganda. Most of it wasn't true. Yet, people embraced it and believed it as if it were true because they did not believe their government would lie to them and they did not have a free press.

Proof of this is in one of the best books I have ever read. It was by Bruno Manz titled, *A MIND IN PRISON* The Memoir of a Son and Soldier of the Third Reich. In the book he talks about all of the propaganda he and his family were exposed to during the Nazi regime. It was everywhere. Even the youth were indoctrinated as members of the Hitler Youth. But the most telling thing for many who have read this book is about after the war. When the Nuremberg Trials began and the information about the Holocaust began to emerge, many in Germany refused to believe it, including his father. Their minds had been so poisoned over the years by constant Nazi propaganda, they simply could not see or believe the truth. One of the regrets Manz had in life concerned his father. To the day his father died, Manz could not convince him of the truth. The hatred and vitriol embedded in him by Nazi propaganda over a period of fifteen years was too much to overcome. His father went to his grave believing the Jews had caused World War II and he never believed the Nazis had perpetrated and orchestrated the Holocaust (Manz).

When someone today says that's fake news, take a deep breath and try and verify. Make sure it is not propaganda. Listen to your inner voice and if you find out it is not true, be mature enough to accept the real truth.

Scary isn't it? That fascist propaganda techniques are alive and well in America in the twenty-first century.

Also, when you hear political leaders sometimes call for censorship of the press or refer to them as "fake news," be cautious. While we might all agree the press/media can be a pain at times, do we really want to give up this right? Do we really want the government or all the network medias to censor or control what we read, hear, and see?

Our founding fathers gave us this important civil liberty. It is our responsibility to see it remains intact for our children and future generations.

Freedom to Assemble

Bill of Rights, Amendment I, ratified December 15, 1791

"...the right of the people peaceably to assemble, and to petition the government for a redress of grievances" (The Bill of Rights: A Transcription).

Since civilization began, rulers and governments have been uncomfortable with allowing people to assemble. Such meetings most likely at times deteriorated into violence and open civil war in which people tried to force the ruler to accept their demands or tried to remove/replace the ruler with someone who favored their ideas.

A good case in point was the famous *Magna Carta*, signed by English barons, lords, churchmen, and of course the infamous King John of England. This document is considered one of the most important documents in history because the barons were able to force King John to address their grievances by signing the charter. Furthermore, it was accomplished without bloodshed on that day in the meadow at Runnymede, between Windsor and Staines, on the fifteenth of June 1215 (Medieval Sourcebook: Magna Carta 1215).

Another case was that of William Penn in England. In 1670, William Penn began speaking in public about his religious (Quaker) ideas. As such the crowds became larger and larger. Uncomfortable with this, the crown had Penn arrested and put in jail for gathering unlawful assemblies. Once again, the king most likely was worried about large gatherings which might be used to try and overthrow either him or his government. Eventually, Penn was found not guilty in a resulting trial. However, this event historically was long remembered by Englishmen who advocated for freedom of assembly (The Freedom of Assembly Clause).

This was a very important human right to our founding fathers. In colonial times, the government often denied people the right to assemble, even if it was in a peaceful way. Those in charge were always worried assembling would get out of control. As far back as ten years prior to the Revolutionary War, Englishmen in the colonies drafted petition after petition and assembled to present them to various governors. Unfortunately, King George III either ignored or denied most of the requests. This too left a bad taste in the minds of Englishmen. Imagine how they felt when they assembled at the Governor's mansion to give a petition, destined for King George III to consider giving them representation in Parliament. Remember the saying, "no taxation without representation." Well, once again, King George III refused to allow the colonists to have any input or representation in Parliament. "Not Good," as a good friend would say.

Our own history, once the country was founded, is also full of peaceful assemblies and marches. We could make the argument that women's suffrage (the right to vote) might never have come about without the many marches they engaged in to win the vote. And, what about the temperance movement. Their marches resulted in the passing and the ratification on 16 January 1919, of the XVIII Amendment.

"After one year from the ratification of this article, ...the manufacture, sale, or transportation of intoxicating liquors...is hereby prohibited" (The Bill of Rights: A Transcription).

Unfortunately for those who voted to ratify this Amendment, things didn't work out. The prohibition of alcohol gave rise to serious criminal activity in the manufacture, and distribution of alcohol. The amendment was eventually repealed by the ratification of *The Twenty-first Amendment*, December 5, 1933 (The Bill of Rights: A Transcription).

And what about the Vietnam War. Many of us grew up during this war. Many favored U.S. involvement in the beginning. However, as time went by, millions of people poured into the streets to protest involvement in the war. There is no doubt in the minds of those who lived thru these peaceful demonstrations, for the most part, that they led to President Nixon eventually withdrawing U.S. forces from Vietnam.

Freedom of assembly is just as important today as it ever was. It remains a way for people to express likes or dislikes of government policy. It's a tradition that we as Americans take full advantage of when the need arises.

The Right to Bear Arms

Bill of Rights, Amendment II, ratified December 15, 1791

The second amendment was passed and then ratified on December 15, 1791. It said,

> "A well-regulated Militia, being necessary to the security of a free State, the right of the people to keep and bear Arms, shall not be infringed"
> (The Bill of Rights: A Transcription).

This is a tough one, although common sense might dictate otherwise. This civil right gives citizens the right to own firearms. It's perfectly logical that our founding fathers would have put this civil right in the *Bill of Rights* because they had just come through some trying times, including the American Revolution. And, had it not been for militia during that time period, the United States may never have won their independence from England. In addition, everyone needed a firearm, especially on the frontiers, for protection and for hunting. Without a firearm it would have been very difficult to put food on the table in frontier territory.

Today there are no frontiers. Yet, there are still reasons why people should be allowed to own some type of firearm. There is the use of a firearm to protect your home and family should someone try to break into your house to steal something or to do bodily harm. There is also the argument for recreational use...target shooting. Many people enjoy going out to a firing range and shooting their weapon at a target.

People argue it is too easy for mentally deranged or challenged people to have possession of a weapon and use it on someone innocent. Guns are also used by gangs in cities to wage war on other gangs. In the process, innocent civilians, including children, often are accidently killed in the exchange of gun fire.

Whichever side you take, the discussions on the second amendment can get rather heated. One side argues for unlimited rights to buy any type of firearm today. The other side argues for increased background checks and restrictions on the type of firearms a citizen can buy. Both sides have valid points but clearly something needs to be done. Too many people are losing their life by gunshots, especially in metropolitan areas. That includes people being shot by police when they don't even have a gun on them or a gun in their car. Later, we will address some statistics on this and throw out some possible reform ideas. For now, let's just say, it is a very controversial civil right in today's world.

No quartering of troops in personal homes

Bill of Rights, Amendment III, ratified December 15, 1791

> "No Soldier shall, in time of peace be quartered in any house, without the consent of the Owner, nor in time of war, but in a manner to be prescribed by law" (The Bill of Rights: A Transcription).

In this amendment we see the Enlightenment Idea which emerged as far back as 1628 with the *Petition of Right*. If you recall, this was *Article VI*. Englishmen objected to often being asked to feed and house soldiers of the king during a campaign or war.

Not much to say about this one. No doubt people today would feel the same way. But to be sure, our founding fathers put it right in the *Bill of Rights*. And, to this day, few would argue for this right to be changed.

The Right of People to be Secure in their Persons ...no unreasonable searches and or seizures

Bill of Rights, Amendment IV

> "The right of the people to be secure in their persons, houses, papers and effects, against unreasonable searches and seizures, shall not be violated, and no Warrants shall issue, but upon probable cause, supported by Oath or affirmation, and particularly describing the place to be searched, and the persons or things to be seized" (The Bill of Rights: A Transcription).

Again, we see the influence of the *Magna Carta* of 1215 and the *Petition of Right* of 1628 in this amendment. Today, few would argue to change this right. It is well established in American law that law enforcement must prove to a judge there is probable cause that someone violated a law in order to obtain a legal search warrant.

Capital Punishment / Due Process of Law / Double Jeopardy / Pleading the Fifth

Bill of Rights, Amendment V

"No person shall be held to answer for a capital, or otherwise infamous crime, unless on a presentment or indictment of a Grand Jury, except in cases arising in the land or naval forces, or in the Militia, when in actual service in time of War or public danger; nor shall any person be subject for the same offense to be twice put in jeopardy of life or limb; nor shall be compelled in any criminal case to be a witness against himself, nor be deprived of life, liberty, or property, without due process of law; nor shall private property be taken for public use without just compensation" (The Bill of Rights: A Transcription).

These concepts in *Amendment V* are extremely important to anyone who has been in trouble with the law. The first says no one can be thrown into jail by a powerful leader (in the time of our founding fathers, a king) or a government without first seeking an indictment from a Grand Jury (a jury of peers). This means before you can be arrested for a capital or infamous crime, the government must prove to a jury of peers that there is enough evidence available to indicate crime was committed and you should stand trial for that crime. This seems commonplace today but in the time of our founding fathers, people could be thrown in jail at the whim of a powerful leader or the local government. The only exception to this is in a time of war or public danger.

Concept number two is also an important civil right. If a person is tried for a capital or infamous crime and found by a jury to be not guilty, a powerful leader or government cannot bring forth additional evidence and seek to try that person again for the same offense they were previously found not guilty. If they could, can you imagine how corrupted officials might bring forth questionable evidence just so you could be put in jail or be executed, despite being found not guilty of that crime initially.

We see the third civil right come into play a lot in politics and law. People who have been involved in a crime, but the government has been unable to prove guilt, will take the fifth amendment when called to testify. This simply means a powerful leader or a government cannot make you say something during an inquiry that would implicate you as part of a crime. The government must prove such an accusation and obtain a warrant for your arrest. In other words, there is a legal process one must go through before you have a day in court. To do so would be to illegally deprive you possibly of your life, your liberty, or your property. These are the unalienable rights our founding fathers fought so hard to establish in America.

During the 2016 election, it became common to hear those in attendance at a political rally chant, "Lock her up." Of course, the people were referring to the candidate's opponent. Yet, if you asked anyone at that rally if they minded being locked up without due process, the answers would have undoubtedly been colorful with a result of, "No, you can't do that." So why did Americans want to lock up a political opponent without providing due process? It's just not American to do so.

While most Americans would never want to give up their right of due process, there are times when Americans are willing to give up some of their liberty. An example of this occurred during the war against Osama bin Laden and terrorism. After the attacks on 9/11, Americans were willing to allow a kind of wiretapping of phone records to try and prevent any more terrorist attacks in the future. *The Patriot Act* was passed and signed by President George W. Bush, which allowed limited wiretapping. Eventually the bill expired and was not renewed because generally Americans do not want the government listening in on their phone conversations. It would be a violation of their liberty.

The last concept in the 5th Amendment refers to a legal concept called eminent domain. This is perhaps the most controversial concept in this amendment. It also comes into play at times when the government wants to take someone's land to build a highway. In order to do that, the government must go to court and obtain a ruling for eminent domain which allows them to take your property to build that road but only if you are paid fair compensation. The government cannot simply take your land and give you nothing in return.

There are thousands of legal eminent domain cases on record but recently, the ones that are the most interesting concern landowners along the southern border. The current administration wants to build a wall along much of the southern border of the United States to control people crossing into the United States illegally from Mexico. Seemingly, most people do not want to spend the money to build such a wall and that includes Texans who own property along the southern border.

Currently, many Texans are fighting cases of eminent domain brought against them by the United States government in their efforts to buy their land to build a wall.

These cases sometime take years to legally resolve. In addition, the United States Congress has no desire to fund (provide money) the building of a wall. Between the Texans resisting the government takeover of their land and the Congress refusing to fund such an endeavor, it remains to be seen if the government can prove in a court of law that building a wall is for the betterment of America.

Right to a speedy and public trial, by an impartial jury

United States Constitution, *Bill of Rights*, Amendment VI, Ratified 15 December 1791

"In all criminal prosecutions, the accused shall enjoy the right to a speedy and public trial, by an impartial jury of the state and district wherein the crime shall have been committed" (The Bill of Rights: A Transcription).

The idea of the right to a speedy and public trial, as well as other ideas eventually found their way into various documents in America and Europe thanks to one of the leading advocates for criminal justice reform. Cesare Beccaria was a famous Italian philosopher. It was Beccaria who dedicated his life to promoting a better criminal justice system. Eventually, many of his ideas were codified into law after the publication of his book *On Crimes and Punishments*, 1774.

In this landmark publication, Beccaria discussed the importance of ending inhumane cruelty in the criminal justice systems throughout Europe. His goal was to influence people to the extent governments might pass more human, just laws which would concentrate on improving not only the criminal justice system but society as well. Some of his enlightenment ideas included a belief that torture was cruel and barbaric. He also felt there should be an established punishment for each type of crime and that people "must be proven guilty in the courts prior to punishment" (Cesare Beccaria; What are Cesare Beccaria's Beliefs).

Cesare
Beccaria
(Marquis of Gualdrasco
and Villareggio)
(1738-1794)

The idea the punishment should fit and deter further crime

United States Constitution, Bill of Rights, Amendment VIII, Ratified 15 December 1791

"Excessive bail shall not be required, nor excessive fines imposed, nor cruel and unusual punishments inflicted" (The Bill of Rights: A Transcription).

Below are several examples of how America's justice system has struggled of late to adhere to both the sixth and the eighth amendment in the *Bill of Rights*. These are dangerous signs America is veering off the path our founding fathers set for us.

The first case involves ripping children out of the arms of their immigrant parents at the southwestern border of the United States. Then, putting them in cages until they are relocated to places around the United States. Their parents are told they are not even allowed to talk with their children, and some have been deported prior to their day in court. Worse, there have been articles online highlighting the fact the government may never be able to reunite deported parents with their children. They simply do not know where the parents are, nor did they keep proper records concerning the children.

Did this happen in America?…Yes. Is this yet another example of cruel and unusual punishment, a violation of *Amendment VIII* of the *Bill of Rights*? And what happened to a speedy and public trial. It would appear these immigrants were denied their day in court prior to being deported. In fact, not only were they denied their day in court and this appears to be cruel and unusual punishment, this borders on crimes against humanity. We will address this in more depth when we discuss immigration later. For now, let's just say violations of the constitution and the *Bill of Rights* are now occurring more frequently in America. Is this really who we have become? Why weren't a million people in the southwest or the U.S. protesting this? Why weren't the border security agents/managers arrested for violation of U.S. law? Show me the law that allows children to be separated from their parents for no just cause? Every Border Security Agent who did this knew they were in violation of the law, especially if the parents told them they were seeking asylum. Where is our justice system? Again, is this who we are now?

Another example of the crime not fitting the punishment might involve a child or youth who did a foolish thing like shop-lift a small item from a store? Fortunately, they were caught, and it scared him or her so much they would never do that again. But what if when they appeared before a judge or magistrate, they were fined $10,000 when the item cost less than $5.00. Or, the judge sentenced your son or daughter to ten years in prison. Do you think this was a fair judgement? Did the punishment fit or deter further crime? Everywhere today we see people at some level of government trying to impose excessive fines.

Case in point...the state of Indiana recently arrested a gentleman for selling about $400 worth of heroin (an illegal drug). The state then turned around and tried to confiscate the gentleman's Land Rover which he purchased for $42,000. In a landmark unanimous ruling, the United States Supreme Court ruled that the Eighth Amendment's protection against excessive fines also applies to state and local jurisdictions (Wolf). Ruth Bader Ginsburg, representing the United States Supreme Court, wrote the majority opinion. In her opinion she stated,

> "This safeguard, we hold, is fundamental to our scheme of ordered liberty." Ginsburg went on to say, "for good reason, the protection against excessive fines has been a constant shield throughout Anglo-American history. Exorbitant tolls undermine other constitutional liberties...Excessive fines can be used, for example, to retaliate against or chill the speech of political enemies" (SUPREME COURT OF THE UNITED STATES Syllabus TIMBS v. INDIANA).

In the days of our founding fathers, gross injustices occurred regularly. People were not often afforded the right to a speedy or public trial. France is a good example of this. Prior to the revolution in 1789, a person could have been imprisoned in the Bastille by the king at any time. Also, many people suffered in the Bastille for years before they were given a proper trial. Some never got a trial or ever got out of the Bastille. It is no wonder that after the French Revolution, the people hated the Bastille and what it represented so much that they tore down every stone of the Bastille.

The Tower of London was probably not much better in England. However, the English idea of justice was far more advanced in England than in France. Thus, the tower survived, and people can visit it today in London.

These enlightenment ideas were codified in our founding documents to prevent gross injustices in America. Yet Americans constantly have to be on guard for human rights violations.

Another case in point involved a young man, twenty-two years old was arrested in New York City in the spring of 2010. He was sixteen at the time. Allegedly he stole a backpack. Upon his arraignment, he was incarcerated at New York's Rikers Island prison. Eventually, the charges were dropped but not before he spent three years at Rikers Island, sometimes in solitary confinement. In addition, the guards often beat him for no reason, (Glenza, Abuse of teen...) except they probably thought he was a thief. Or, perhaps they just did it for enjoyment. Also, according to his mother, he was starved and not allowed to have a shower for two weeks at a time. Is this not cruel and unusual punishment which violates constitutional *Amendment VIII*? Who knows why people do such things, regardless of what century they live in?

In 2013, his charges were dismissed by prosecutors, no doubt for a lack of evidence, and he was released. Finally, he was able to return to his home in the Bronx.

During this entire time, the young man maintained his innocence. More importantly, he never went to trial. He was never afforded the opportunity to prove his innocence (Glenza, Kalif...). The scars that were left on this young man never healed. Both in prison and while home he struggled for his life. Several times he tried to commit suicide. After each unsuccessful attempt at suicide, he tried to rebuild his life with the help of others. In fact, someone paid for his tuition to attend Bronx Community College. But every time it looked as if he was getting his life back together, he relapsed into paranoia, shock, and depression. This went on for over two years until finally, he lost his battle. His mother found him hanging on June 6, 2015 (Gonnerman).

This young man's experiences in New York City went against everything he had ever been taught about America in a public school. Some would ask after hearing this story, did this happen in America? …Yes. Was the treatment he received after his arrest constitutional? …NO; Should this have happened in America? …NO, NEVER EVER. But it did! And where was the outcry from informed citizens? Why wasn't there a million people marching in the streets until this abuse of the justice system was rectified?

Activities like these happened all the time in the colonies in 1776. In fact, there are countries today where this still happens, including the United States. I suspect if we looked long and hard, we could find numerous examples of excessive fines.

Why, for example, do the federal laws contradict state laws when it comes to marijuana? Under federal law, anyone caught selling or using marijuana should be incarcerated and given a trial. Yet, some cities, even entire states now have legalized marijuana for both medical and recreational purposes. How is that fair to someone who lives in a state that would incarcerate them or impose an excessive fine upon them when in fact, if they lived in Colorado, they could literally walk into a marijuana dispensary store and buy it in many forms?

Just like in France in 1800, our legal system needs an overhaul. Napoleon overhauled it in France with his *Napoleonic Code*, which laid the groundwork for the French legal system today. Our system on the other hand is a hodgepodge of various laws between the federal and state governments which, in many ways, do not appear to be coordinated. It is a good thing the U.S. Supreme Court performs the job of reaffirming human rights inherent in American culture

Chapter 5

Additional Human Rights and Civil Liberties Americans Believe In

No Slavery

Amendment XIII, Ratified December 6, 1865

> "Neither slavery nor involuntary servitude, except
> as a punishment for crime whereof the party
> shall have been duly convicted, shall exist within
> the United States, or any place subject to the
> jurisdiction"
> (The Bill of Rights: A Transcription).

Not much to say on this one. The idea that no one should be a slave goes all the way back to 539 B.C. We know this because archeologists discovered the "Cyrus Cylinder" in modern day Iraq in 1879. It was a baked clay tablet, written in the Akkadian language. Once they deciphered it, they realized it was a kind of history incorporating certain human rights for citizens. This clay cylinder is considered "the world's first charter of human rights" (A Brief History of Human Rights the Cyrus Cylinder, 539 B.C.).

Cyrus the Great was the first king of Persia. His armies conquered Babylon in 539 B.C. Nothing is unusual about that. History is full of rulers conquering other lands. What he did next though began an evolutionary development of codifying laws for subjects in a document for all to see and follow.

The *Cyrus Cylinder* promulgated:

- All slaves were freed.
- In the future, slavery was prohibited in his realm.
- All people had the right to choose a religion they wished to practice.
- Racial equality was established (A Brief History of Human Rights the Cyrus Cylinder, 539 B.C.).

This idea of codifying certain human rights eventually spread to India, Greece, then Rome. And, of course after the fall of Rome the ideas did not die. Many ideas lived on to emerge in England in the year 1215 with the signing of the Magna Carta. In America, it took a long five year civil war, from 1860 to 1865, where almost one million people died before slaves became free and slavery was outlawed in the United States.

Unfortunately, slavery still exists in the world today. It is a constant battle to fight against nations and groups that want to enslave people. Fortunately, The United Nations is also against slavery. It is not only an American Human Right but a United Nations Human Right as well. United Nations Article #4 states,

"No one shall be held in slavery or servitude; slavery and the slave trade shall be prohibited in all their forms" (United Nations Declaration of Human Rights).

Slavery today takes many forms. For example, when people pay money to come to America and once here are chained up or held captive in a house to be factory workers. That's an example of modern-day slavery. Fortunately, in the U.S. there are laws against such actions. Hopefully, no one would want to turn the clock back to make slavery legal, period.

1789: Declaration of the Rights of Man and of the Citizen

This famous French document was written and adopted roughly two years after the American constitution was written. Nevertheless, we can see in its articles many of the human rights and civil liberties championed by Americans. And, while they are not directly in our constitution, they have been since codified in both legislative and common laws in America.

First, in Articles 4 and 5, and 10 and 11, the French specifically refine the rights of liberty, freedom of speech, and freedom of religion.

- Liberty consists in the power to do anything that does not injure others; accordingly, the exercise of the rights of each man has no limits except those that secure the enjoyment of these same rights to the other members of society. These limits can be determined only by law (Anderson 59).

- The law has only the rights to forbid such actions as are injurious to society (Anderson 59).

- No one ought to be disturbed on account of his opinions, even religious, provided their manifestation does not derange the public order established by law (Anderson 59).

- The free communication of ideas and opinions is one of the most precious of the rights of man; every citizen can then freely speak, write, and print, subject to responsibility for the abuse of this freedom in the cases determined by law (Anderson 60).

In these articles, we can see American law which prohibits people from doing something which could injure others, either physically or mentally. The example of yelling "fire" in a public assembly when there is no fire, is a perfect example of the limits of both liberty and freedom of speech. And while most everyone agrees with this, it becomes a hot topic today when we talk about recent hate speech activity on social media, especially regarding religion or politics.

Should hate speech, which can be mentally harmful to people or can motivate people to do horrendous things, fall under the category of injuring others? Should there be a law against a person who displays a confederate flag in public or on their clothing? Should a person be fined or even go to jail for participating in such acts of hate? These and more are tricky questions.

Almost no one today would question arresting a person who crosses the line by going into a place of worship and shooting/killing innocent civilians worshipping. We do have laws against such actions. Yet, when we talk of mental harm inflicted on others via the internet or social media today or even print, we might get a debate. Some would argue people should be allowed to engage in such activities. People are free to do so in a country that guarantees freedom of speech. But remember, this was not the intent of founding fathers, nor the intent of the French or many other western cultures. On the contrary, if someone's actions are injurious to another person or persons, then many would argue such actions should be outlawed in today's world.

The danger of spreading hate, given the technology to transmit hate speech and ideas worldwide, is very real today. Did you know that spreading hate speech/ideas on the internet or social media is a stage of genocide? When someone labels a person a name or calls them an animal, like cockroaches, that is hate speech, which is considered "Dehumanization," the fourth stage of genocide (Stanton). People in a society don't generally wake up one morning and decide to kill all the members of a group, unless of course they are mentally ill. Historically, that's not how genocide works. The idea is spread through stages and one of those stages occurs when people openly start referring to people in a group they hate as animals. Why would people participate in stages of genocide in any form? Perhaps in an effort to discourage such activity in America, we should think about how to encourage people to change so they do not participate in hate speech or engage in sending pictures of people over the internet or social media portraying them as savages or animals.

1864: The Geneva Conventions

Years later, Americans bought into the ideas promoted at the Geneva Conventions. These too have become part of American culture when it comes to the rules of warfare and more. From 1863 to 1977, numerous nations have met in Geneva Switzerland, the United States being one of them. The purpose of the meetings was to address in writing, atrocities committed against wounded soldiers and civilians, including children during a time of war. Some of the items addressed include:

1. Issues dealing with the wounded in war.

2. Providing relief to the wounded in war without any distinction as to their nationality.

3. How to handle children in a time of war.
   These include:

   • According to the information on the Geneva Convention website,

"Children should be well cared for and educated, and the following is prohibited.

- Taking hostages
- Terrorism
- Pillage
- Slavery
- Group punishment
- Humiliating or degrading treatment"
(History.com Editors Geneva Convention)

4. Neutrality (inviolability) of medical personnel and medical establishments and units.

5. The distinctive sign of the Red Cross. Furthermore, "in 2005, a protocol was created to recognize the symbol of the red crystal—in addition to the red cross, the red crescent and the red shield of David—as universal emblems of identification and protection in armed conflicts" (History.com Editors Geneva Convention).

Is there anyone today who would take exception to the humane treatment of children outlined by the Geneva Conventions? It is highly unlikely.

Elimination Of Torture

One other item is the debate over torture today. If you are on the borderline, ask yourself a very simple question. Do you favor the enemy torturing your child someday who is a soldier in the U.S. armed forces and has been captured by the enemy?

It is doubtful the answer to that question is yes. It's hard to imagine anyone among us who wants to see a loved one, whether a civilian or a soldier, caught up in war, either captured by the enemy, killed, tortured or abused? For most, common sense says no because we are Americans. While we don't think of our agreement with the Geneva Conventions as something that makes us American, in fact it is. This also means that anyone who violates these agreed upon international rules of behavior on how to treat humans during war, also violates American values and international law and should be punished appropriately.

In the U.S. we are protected from such atrocities and bestial treatment by our constitution and our laws/court decisions. In addition, there are also international laws of which the U.S. is a signatory country. Below are just a few examples cited in Cohn's article, "Under U.S. Law Torture is Always Illegal."

- The Convention Against Torture and Other Cruel, Inhumane or Degrading Treatment or Punishment (Convention Against Torture and Other Cruel, Inhuman Or Degrading Treatment or Punishment)
- The Geneva Conventions
- The War Crimes Act
  (18 U.S. Code Section 2441. War Crimes)
- The Torture Statue
  (18 U.S. Code Section 2340A. Torture)
- The U.S. Army Field Manual

While we are on the subject of torture, waterboarding today, is considered a form of torture. When Vice-President Dick Cheney authorized waterboarding of U.S. prisoners, he was breaking not only U.S. law but international law as well. Yet, he was never brought to justice, nor were the people who were waterboarding prisoners. How is this possible? What is the purpose of having laws if we are not going to enforce them?

Part of the problem lies in the Executive Branch. As Cohn points out, "Under the doctrine of command responsibility, used at Nuremberg and enshrined in the Army Field Manual, commanders, all the way up the chain of command to the commander in chief, can be liable for war crimes if they knew or should have known their subordinates would commit them and they did nothing to stop or prevent it. The Bush officials ordered the torture after seeking legal cover from lawyers" (Cohn).

What we see here again is the Executive Branch finding people in the Justice Department who would spin and twist the wording of our laws/court cases and international laws to torture people at Guantanamo and abroad. If you don't believe this, read the Open the Government Shadow Report about what the United States did regarding waterboarding people. It's not for the faint of heart but the very last paragraph says it all.

"If other countries adopted the United States' view that evidence of torture by the security services was a state secret, and victim's descriptions of their own treatment was classified, how could the prohibition on torture ever be enforced" (The Impact of Executive Branch Secrecy on the United States' Compliance with the Convention Against Torture and other Cruel Inhumane or Degrading Treatment or Punishment)?

Either we are the good guys or not. If we must act like the bad guys in order to win, then maybe we don't deserve to win. What's the point of winning if you don't have anything better to give people?

The bottom line once again is we need to think very seriously about separating the Justice Department from the Executive Branch and allow U.S. marshals, prosecutors, and the FBI, opportunities to enforce the laws of this land

and its treaties. And, if we cannot bring ourselves to punish our own leaders, then we must allow the international community to punish leaders. That means we need to finally join the ICC (International Criminal Court in the Hague, Netherlands).

1948: The United Nations Declaration of Human Rights

Elenore Roosevelt, wife of President Franklin D. Roosevelt, was the first lady of the United States from 1932 to 1945. During that time, the President could barely walk. Because he contracted polio disease years earlier, he had been left a cripple. Most of the time he was in a wheelchair. Sometimes he relied on his wife to be his eyes and ears by asking her to travel places and talk with people.

In 1948, Elenore was asked to help develop a universal declaration of human rights for the new United Nations. She accepted and turned out to be instrumental in the development of this doctrine. Who better to have input from than the wife of the President of the United States?

The document was completed and ratified unanimously in 1948 by all members of the United Nations. It is known as the *United Nations Declaration of Human Rights*. As you can probably guess, many of the human rights and civil liberties in the United States, found their way into the U.N. document, despite the wording being somewhat different. The enlightenment concepts are the very same. There are also other interesting rights in the document that most Americans have come to support. If we examine legislative laws and common laws, we see almost all of them reaffirmed in American jurisprudence. Below is a brief discussion of some of those additional rights.

Article 1 states, "all men are born free and equal in dignity and rights. They are endowed with reason and conscience and should act towards one another in a spirit of brotherhood" (Universal Declaration of Human Rights).

It is the second part of this article which is interesting. Perhaps because it was so close to the end of World War II in which the world witnessed the SS/Nazis committing horrible crimes against humanity, that the authors felt compelled to put the second sentence in this article. It also may be related to America being predominately a nation of Christians at the time. It reminds me of the Christian saying, "do unto others as you would have them do unto you." Either way, you can tell it is a belief we as Americans, we hope most Americans, hold dear to their hearts. Why else would people be so upset with politicians who have referred to immigrant groups arriving as "rapists and criminals." Referring to any group like this is simply not American.

In addition, in *Article #6*, "everyone has the right to recognition everywhere as a person before the law" (Universal Declaration of Human Rights). Then, in *Article #7*, "all are equal before the law and are entitled without any discrimination to equal protection of the law" (Universal Declaration of Human Rights). There should be no distinction made between citizens of a country. If you travel, for example, you have the right to be treated fairly in a foreign country. If you are an immigrant seeking asylum in another country, you have the right to be treated fairly in another country.

Another article, #12, talks about, "No one shall be subjected to arbitrary interference with his privacy, family, home or correspondence, nor to attacks upon his honor and reputation. Everyone has the right to the protections of the law against such interference or attacks" (Universal Declaration of Human Rights). Perhaps, this is why so many people are disgusted with politics. It seems every time you turn around, politicians are calling each other names or insulting the honor of another politician. If people didn't believe in this idea, they wouldn't care. Yet, that's not the case. So, again, this belief we are all entitled to our home, honor, etc., should be another factor that makes us American.

Concerning work, *Article #23* addresses several ideas that Americans have come to believe in. Almost everyone would agree with the first item under *Article #23*, "everyone has the right to work, to free choice of employment, to just and favorable conditions of work and to protection against unemployment" (Universal Declaration of Human Rights). Here we can understand how OSHA (Occupational Safety and Health Administration) came about. People simply came to believe they were entitled to work in an environment that was safe. In time, they forced their representatives and senators to enact legislation to these ends.

The same holds true for unemployment. Today most states have some type of unemployment agency whereby people receive some type of help in the event they lose their job. Americans would probably be unhappy were the state governments to do away with unemployment provisions.

The third article under #23 talks about having the "right to just and favorable remuneration ensuring for himself and his family an existence worthy of human dignity, and supplemented, if necessary, by other means of social protection" (Universal Declaration of Human Rights). Here again, we see the need for a safety net of social benefits. We also see an argument being made for equal pay for equal work. We do have some laws regarding this and most likely if you asked one hundred Americans, do they believe in this as a right, the answer for the majority would be yes. Unfortunately, we still have some work to do for women, minorities, migrant workers, and others who often do not receive a just and favorable remuneration for their work.

Most likely, no one would disagree with #4 under *Article #23*. It talks about everyone having a right to join a trade union "for the protection of their interests" (Universal Declaration of Human Rights). In this, the argument might center around any requirements forcing a person to join a union.

Article #24 we have all come to believe in and enjoy. It states, "Everyone has the right to rest and leisure, including reasonable limitation of working hours and periodic holidays with pay" (Universal Declaration of Human Rights). In America there are numerous laws both federal and state about working hours and holidays.

In *Article #25*, subsection 1, we can see President Franklin D. Roosevelt's philosophy on social benefits. It states, "Everyone has the right to a standard of living adequate for the health and well-being of himself and of his family, including food, clothing, housing and medical care and necessary social services, and the right to security in the event of unemployment, sickness, disability, widowhood, old age or other lack of livelihood in circumstances beyond his control" (Universal Declaration of Human Rights). During the Great Depression, Roosevelt signed legislation after legislation to help put people back to work so they could provide food and clothing for their family. In addition, he signed into law Social Security to make sure older citizens who lost all the money when a bank collapsed, did not have to live the rest of their lives in destitute poverty. Years later, Medicare was enacted to help senior citizens pay for their medical bills and prescriptions. The only piece to the puzzle left is a basic healthcare program for every citizen in the United States. Slowly people are beginning to realize that you cannot pursue happiness if you don't have medical coverage. And, that means it too is a human right. In the section on healthcare, we will provide some ideas on how to reform our current healthcare system in the hopes that one day everyone will be covered by a basic healthcare program in America.

Article #26 concerns education. For the most part, most everyone would agree with the U.N. thinking on this subject. "Everyone has a right to education…free, at least in the elementary and fundamental states. Elementary education shall be compulsory. Technical and professional education shall be made generally available and higher education shall be equally accessible to all on the basis of merit" (Universal Declaration of Human Rights). Again, hopefully most all Americans believe in this right.

Furthermore, "education shall be directed to the full development of the human personality and to the strengthening of respect for human rights and fundamental freedoms. It shall promote understanding, tolerance, and friendship among all nations, racial or religious groups, and shall further the activities of the United Nations for the maintenance of peace." Parents also "have a right to choose the kind of education that shall be given to their children" (Universal Declaration of Human Rights). For the most part, there are few Americans who would argue with any of this right.

America has been a beacon of Human Rights and Civil Liberties since its beginning in 1776. It is not surprising many of the U.N. Human Rights either came from America or fit right in with our unique American culture. More importantly, how do we sustain this unique culture. How do we protect our precious Human Rights and Civil Liberties, as well as the ability of our government to protect us from foreign powers and the ability of our government to provide future needed goods and services? Hopefully, we can answer these questions and more in the section that follows regarding important needed reforms.

Sustaining our Unique American Culture

C hapter 6

Important Needed Reforms

Have you ever wondered what life is all about? Is it about good vs. evil as many great religions of the world preach? Or, is it about those who have the wealth doing everything possible to hold onto their wealth and keep those who do not have the wealth from getting a piece of the good life like Marx and Engle preached?

Perhaps, it is a little of both at times. Clearly, the French Revolution of 1789, the Mexican Revolution of 1910, the Bolshevik Revolution of 1918, and the China Revolution of 1948 were a result of the rich controlling ninety-eight percent of all the wealth in society. This is not to say evil wasn't committed during these revolutions. It is to say the dominant force was the disparity of income between those at the top and those below in society. Then there was the Holocaust in Europe during W.W. II. We could easily argue this was a result of hatred and evil.

So, how do we keep these types of human struggles from tearing apart American society? How do we protect and sustain America's unique culture, including those important human rights and civil liberties?

Years ago, things were getting out of hand in America. A few Americans were becoming extremely wealthy while others barely got by. This time period became known as the Gilded Age. Fortunately, a few social activists, known as the Muckrakers in the early twentieth century, exposed the ills of society. Frank Norris wrote about the ills of the railroads and grain speculators. Theodore Dreiser wrote about the lack of "social responsibility among the rich" (Graebner, Fite & White 858). Jack London wrote about the failures of the classical Laissez-faire economic system. And, Upton Sinclair detailed the evils of the meat-packing industry in his writings (Graebner, Fite & White 858).

Of course, none of these writers had all the answers we seek. Yet, time marches on. In the case of the Muckrakers they were able to make a difference. Safety measures were enacted for the work place which helped curb the growing exploitation of labor by the rich and powerful. The lesson to learn from the Muckrakers is we must continually strive to assess and improve society. In the end, good always triumphs over evil. Sometimes the rich and powerful come to see that it is better to create a more just society and a better world than to tear everything down.

Our ancestors were successful in the past. Hopefully, when things settle down in the federal government, we too, can move forward to create a better world for future Americans. We hope we can enact desired changes like term limits that have eluded Americans for so long and eliminate the antiquated Electoral College system.

All of this reminds me of one of my favorite historians... Georg Wilhelm Friedrich Hegel (1770-1831), a European philosopher who lived during the Romantic period in history. His beliefs were complicated, but he felt all periods of history were important. In each period (the thesis), there is a zeitgeist (spirit of the age) and as time goes by an opposing view of society develops (the antithesis...a clash of values and ideas so to speak). Eventually, these two forces the thesis and anti-thesis clash to create a new set of values, (the synthesis) a new zeitgeist. These new values then allow mankind to move forward...to evolve, to develop a better world (Georg Wilhelm Friedrich Hegel).

Perhaps, we are in an antithesis stage today. Everywhere we look the values of old school are clashing with those of post W.W. II. When Barack Obama became our first African-American elected President, many thought we had emerged into a new world, a new zeitgeist (spirit of the age) and synthesis, where everyone is accepted for who they are, and most people play by the rules. Yet, today we see many of our human rights and civil liberties under attack from many sides. It's as if some people want to turn the clock back to 1929. What would that mean?

Well, in 1929, the K.K.K. was at the height of its power. Prior to 1929, there had even been marches down Pennsylvania Avenue in Washington D.C. by the K.K.K. White society in the U.S. was dominant, particularly in the south. Black Americans were living in a segregated world with little hope of being truly free to eat in the same restaurants, drink from the same water fountains as white folk, vote, work at certain jobs, attend the same schools and colleges and universities and much, much more. In the southwestern part of the U.S. there was rampant discrimination against Hispanic Americans and other non-white races. In the west there was discrimination against both Asian Americans and Hispanic Americans. It was the same story just a different minority.

Some thought all this was behind us. Yet, here we are in 2020 with a president who at times acts as if he wants to be a fascist dictator. He repeatedly speaks as if he is the only one in America who has done anything for the country and its people. The use of the word "I" did this and "I" did that is very disconcerting. He even makes comments about "the press is the enemy of the people." That phrase is generally credited to one of the most notorious communist dictators of all time...Joseph Stalin, who butchered thirty-three million people in his day. It's doubtful any American leader wants to butcher anybody. But, all of this has enabled white supremacists to do things that five years ago, would have been unthinkable.

In addition, many societies around the world are also in turmoil. White supremacists and terrorists are empowered more today than ever before because of the internet and social media. At any time, they can go online and chat with other white supremacist and terrorist groups. They can even skype meetings as if all were in attendance. When they get crazed with hate, they sometimes go out and commit hate crimes and crimes against humanity like the Emanuel African Methodist Church shooting June 17, 2015 in Charleston, South Carolina, or the Tree of Life synagogue shooting on October 27, 2018 in the Squirrel Hill neighborhood of Pittsburgh, Pennsylvania or, the massacre in Christchurch, New Zealand on March 15, 2019 at the Al Noor Mosque, and the Linwood Islamic Center, and other places around the world.

Today, America is passing through one of the worst social and political storms experienced in a long time. Many people are not able to enjoy the "good life" for many reasons. Take jobs for example. Yes, there is full employment and the stock market is booming. But, millions and millions of good paying jobs have been lost to cheap labor overseas in the last twenty years. American international corporations have moved, some claim, over 60,000 factories to countries like China, Mexico, Canada, Indonesia, India and other countries where they are paying people $3.50 to $5.00 per hour to work. In China, some young ladies make textiles for $35.00 to $40.00 per week . This has resulted in millions of American workers being unemployed/underemployed in the United States. That's a big-time problem.

Furthermore, the belief that those factories are going to come home soon and will provide people with $10 to $20 per hour jobs or more, is just another smoke and mirrors claim perpetrated on working Americans by con artist politicians. While a few companies have come home in the past few years, overall that promise has not materialized to date.

Unfortunately, the government, our economic system and frankly, the American people have allowed all of this to transpire over the past twenty to thirty years. However, all is not lost.

Despite all of the negative events, there are a lot of really positive things happening today. Take technology for example. There are touch screen laptops, smart tablets, smart phones, smart Televisions (TVs), and home assistants that can turn the lights on and off as well as ovens and more. Electronic devices can even order products and food from stores and nearby fast food restaurants. There are cars that can taxi people from one location to another without a driver. Energy is becoming more efficient…with giant windmills dotting the land-scape and solar panels on top of homes and businesses to provide energy for running hot water heaters and more. There are drones now that can deliver products or take a photo from the air or search for missing people or scan for survivors after a natural disaster. In addition, robots are being developed to clean floors, mow grass, and to make production in industry more efficient and less labor intensive than ever before. Socially, gay and lesbian people are allowed to marry. In America, minorities for the most part, enjoy the same rights as white folk. Women have more rights today than ever before and much, much more.

What does all this mean? It means we are again at a crossroads. We are experiencing all this turmoil because we are in an antithesis period in history, struggling with how to move forward. Do we revert to many past practices or do we move forward into a new world, a new synthesis, taking the best of our past world with us while making many, if not all, the needed reforms and more noted herein?

What follows are some suggestions for a discussion on needed reforms. It is not expected everyone will agree with all of them. But, if we can agree on many of them, we can begin the process of creating a better future for all Americans as well as future generations. We can sustain our unique American culture and what it means to be an American in the twenty-first century and beyond for everyone to enjoy.

If you feel we are on the right path, we challenge you to take up our call to reform in the next chapter. Note also, this is not a democratic or republican or independent issue. For these reforms to succeed, we need the majority of all Americans to help, regardless of their political party affiliation. A more detailed discussion on many issues will most likely follow in volume 2 of *A Call To Reform* whereby, based upon your input, we will examine in more depth why these reforms are needed. For now, please review the subsequent suggested important reforms herein.

Reform Ideas for Discussion on Political Parties

One of the greatest threats to the United States is the radicalization of political parties and the electorate. All Americans must work to minimize radicalization if we want our unique American culture to continue. Below are some ideas to consider.

- Encourage all high school seniors to register as independent voters while they are in Social Studies class. Provide students with the forms/computers to register online.
- If they so choose to re-register with a specific party at that time or later, they are free to do so.
- Encourage adults to re-register as independent voters in respective legislative districts.

- Re-educate voters on the purpose of political parties... that is to say, political parties should be responsible for coming up with good candidates to help provide the quality goods and services needed to their state and country. When voters are thinking about who to vote for, they should be thinking **not about their party** but about how a candidate feels about policies and issues confronting the country/state today.

- Once elected, state and federal representatives/senators should be working with others to do what is best for America. They should not be against compromising with others to get things done. It is not about a party maintaining control of a legislature... it is about doing what is best for all Americans, regardless of party. If they don't want to do this, they should not run for public office and people should consider not voting for these types of politicians.

- Re-educate candidates to understand they are not running for office to better themselves. They are running for office to serve in the public sector, to do what is best for America, their state and its citizens.

Reform Ideas for Discussion on the Legislative Branch

Establishing term limits for both the House of Representatives and the Senate would go a long way toward minimizing radical partisan politics. Below are some ideas to consider which also would require a Constitutional change.

Article I. Section 2., **must be changed to allow for,**

- "The House of Representatives shall be composed

of Members chosen," every **Three Years** by a direct vote of the people in a legislative district. Members shall **not serve more than a total of three terms (nine years total)**. Age requirements shall be established by law as times change. Also, perhaps if we extend their time between elections to three years, they may be inclined to get more work done and campaign less.

Article I. Section 3., **must be changed to allow for,**

- The Senate shall be composed of Two Members from each state, chosen" every **Six Years** by a direct vote of the people in a state. Furthermore, members shall **not serve more than two total terms (twelve years total)**. Age requirements shall be established by law as times change.

The ideas listed below could be established by simply changing the laws/procedures in both the House of Representatives and the Senate.

- If a member reaches the **age of eighty** and is still serving in either the U.S. House of Representatives or the U.S. Senate, that member shall **resign their seat forthwith**.
- A piece of legislation should come to the floor for a vote within six months if X amount of majority members sponsor the bill and X amount of minority members also sponsor the bill. No legislative leader should ever be allowed to pigeonhole a bill for more than six months.
- Up or down votes should be taken on all legislation with only amendments added to fine-tune a bill. There can be **no amendments added** that have nothing to do with the bill being voted on. The age-old adage applies, keep it simple stupid!

- A government web site, free of charge and available to all citizens, should be designed to show how each member of the House of Representatives and the Senate voted on any piece of legislation. Total transparency must prevail if you want people to get more involved with their government! This web site should also include the number of bills a member failed to vote on and the annual percentage of those failed votes.

- Any member who fails, within a calendar year, to vote on **less than eighty-five percent** of all the legislation voted upon that year, **shall resign** his or her seat by **February 1 of the following year**. The only exception to this should be if the member was seriously ill but expected to recover soon enough to function normally.

- All special perk programs for members of Congress should be eliminated. Also, when it comes to healthcare, they should have available the same programs as anyone else in America. They can be enrolled in a private healthcare plan or if over the age of 65, Medicare and a private supplemental policy. The same applies for Social Security. The same for retirement…their program should be comparable to what others have in the U.S. Most people have some type of a 401 K plan. And, when they retire from Congress, they should not get special lifetime programs. Almost no one in America has such a thing. Why should they?

- Every year, an amount of money will be set aside in the Federal Budget for use by Congress. The total amount available to Congressional state delegations will be decided, each year, by an approved amount in the annual budget. Once the total amount is decided, the amount each state will have available will be based on the percentage of their population to the whole population of the United States. Then, throughout the year, each state delegation can access their funds by voting as a state delegation (House of Representative and Senate members from a state). Territories would not be eligible for these funds until they become a state.

- An easy to follow government web site will be available on the internet for citizens to follow how their state delegates voted to access project funds.

Reform Ideas for a Discussion on Healthcare

Previously we talked about Thomas Jefferson's proclamation in the *Declaration of Independence* for Life, Liberty and the Pursuit of Happiness. In the modern world it is hard to imagine being able to live your life, be free and pursue happiness, if a person does not have access to healthcare. How is it in a country as wealthy as the United States that all people do not have some type of basic healthcare plan? It has been said before and let's say it again. The United States is the only industrial nation in the western world that does not have some type of basic healthcare plan for all citizens who do not have access to healthcare. It's time to change that.

The recent Democratic Presidential Debates have emphasized how difficult and complicated healthcare can be. So, let's continue to work together to find an acceptable solution to move forward. Below are some ideas to continue the healthcare reform discussion. These ideas are in the category of let's learn to walk before we run and much like the U.N. believes, it is a human right.

"(1) Everyone has the right to a standard of living adequate for the health and well-being of himself and his family, including food, clothing, housing, and medical care and necessary social services, and the right to security in the event of unemployment, sickness, disability, widowhood, old age, or other lack of livelihood in circumstances beyond his control" (U.N. Declarations of Human Rights).

As we continue this discussion, we must also remember, citizens need to continue being responsible for and becoming advocates for their own health. That means asking a lot of questions when you have a doctor's visit and trying to lead a life filled with good health habits. Below are some ideas for you to ponder on healthcare in America.

- Expand Medicare to include anyone age fifty-five years of age or older. Think of this as the Basic Healthcare Right program which will include coverages for wellness, including exercise classes should a person choose to do so (Silver Sneaker), annual checkups, life or death issues like heart attack, stroke, cancer, and more. Also, keep the same coverage provisions that are currently in the *Affordable Care Act*. For example, no one can be denied healthcare because of a pre-existing condition.

Note: Medicare should continue to be structured like it is now whereby people who are currently employed will have the option to register for Medicare once they reach age fifty-five but can choose to stay on their employer's healthcare plan until such time as their employment ends.

- Next, continue to allow insurance companies to sell supplemental plans, advantage plans, or whatever you want to call them, to those people age fifty-five years of age or older on Medicare. This will help cover the twenty percent Medicare does not cover. Also, make this voluntary. If someone feels they don't want to spend the money or feels they don't need this extra coverage…that's ok. If someone can't afford to buy a supplemental plan, allow them to apply for government help to provide this important coverage gap insurance.

If you are fifty-four years of age or younger, coverage will be provided voluntarily either by the government or a private health insurance company through your employer or if it is your choice to purchase a plan. Think of this as a Privilege Healthcare program. This is where employers and individuals can go to a private insurance company or to the government-run electronic marketplace (like what we have now) and purchase a plan for themselves and or their employees. These plans should cover most orthopedic issues like back pain, aches and sprains and elective surgery, such as total knees, hips, shoulders, and back surgery, maladies that are non-cancerous. The plans should also cover bariatric surgeries and some dental issues. These types of pathologies, while they can be quality of life issues, are not usually life or death issues.

- This next idea is controversial. Add a bare-bones, basic government run healthcare program on the government exchange (something like the Medicaid program perhaps). This should ensure that private insurance companies will not engage in price increases through collusion. The very fact this is a near monopoly industry, with very few companies means you have to have a government run healthcare program to keep the companies from raising prices. And, if the private companies cannot compete with the government run healthcare program, this will indicate that perhaps healthcare is a market failure in a relatively free market economy. After all, do entrepreneurs build interstate roads? Do they build massive bridges or provide fire companies or ambulance squads in cities? Do they build ports or even large sports complexes? No, they do not because they can't make a profit building such enterprises. In economics this is called a market failure. This is why the government taxes people, in order to provide these important infrastructures/services in a relatively free market economy to facilitate capitalism. Whether or not people receive healthcare should not hinge on whether the provider makes a profit or not. Maybe it's time for Americans to see healthcare as an industry which provides services that are best for peoples' health and well-being.

- Non-Profit healthcare is perhaps not what it seems. Non-profit hospitals, for example, often make record profits paying upper administrative staff hundreds of millions of dollars. The government needs to begin to regulate this entire process. A non-profit healthcare executive should not make more money than the president of the United States. In today's world that would be $500,000. If you work at a for-profit hospital, you can make all the money you want because the hospital will have to pay taxes on profits.

- Downsize the Veterans Administration (VA) healthcare program. This means closing all VA hospitals and giving veterans a Medicare type card.

This way they will be able to go to any doctor, hospital or urgent care facility of their choice that accepts Medicare. Coverages should also include mental health coverage for Post-Traumatic Stress Disorder (often referred to as PTSD) and other mental challenges.

- Allow insurance companies to bid on administering Medicare and other government run healthcare programs like Medicaid. This will help provide jobs for people in the insurance industry.

- If unemployed and you cannot purchase insurance, you will be eligible for the bare-bones government run healthcare program on the exchange.

- It is your responsibility to purchase healthcare from somewhere. However, if you choose not to have health insurance, then you will no longer be eligible to walk into a hospital or an emergency care unit and ask for their services, unless it is a life-threatening event in which case the hospital will take care of you. Everyone should have some type of healthcare or suffer the consequences.

- Tie the amount taken off a person's paycheck for Medicare to the Consumer Price Index.

  For example, if after a year or two, it is determined that we need to increase the amount of money taken out of a person's paycheck for Medicare, say by two percent, because inflation increased two percent, then the following will be deducted from someone's paycheck...(1.45% * 2%) = 1.479%

- Try to limit the people who are eligible for early Social Security because of disability from work related injuries or mental health disorders. This is not to say everyone in this category is "faking," but a lot seem to be retiring early to get Social Security or Medicare. On the contrary, anyone who can work, should work. Benefits from early Social Security or Medicare can be coordinated with employment, instead of full disability payments. This will help cut down on the costs of these programs. And, it's healthy for people to work and contribute toward their communities as best they can.

- The U.S. government must do whatever it can to decrease the cost of prescription drugs, period!

One last note…using socialism as an excuse to deny millions of people healthcare is another smoke and mirrors tactic. Currently, America is considered economically, a mixed modern economy. As such there are elements of modern-day socialism built into the economy. For example, did you ever stop to think of where Social Security, Medicare, Unemployment Insurance, Medicaid, Workers' Compensation, etc., came from? And, what about the FDIC (Federal Deposit Insurance Corporation) protecting money deposited in a member back up to $250,000 per bank. These are programs/benefits found in modern-day Socialistic countries in Europe and Australia. The only difference in America is there is a high degree of capitalism and a moderate safety net of social programs/benefits. In a pure modern-day socialistic country, you would find a moderate to low degree of capitalism with an extensive safety net of social programs/benefits. Is there anyone in the United States, at least any working middle class people and or retired citizens, who wish to do away with any of these moderate social programs/benefits?

Detailing all this is an infographic. See *A Comparison of the Characteristics of the Big Four Economic Systems* on the following page.

A Comparison of the Characteristics of the Big Four Economic Systems

Communism (No/Little Free Market)	Modern Day Socialism (Moderate Free Market)	Mixed Modern Extensive (Free Market)	Laissez Faire (Free Market)
What's it all about?			
The State / The State	Community 1st / Individuals 2nd	Individuals 1st / Community 2nd	Individuals / Individuals
How does it begin?			
Violent revolution - Wealthy & middle class can lose everything / life	Democracy - Voted in peacefully	Democracy - Voted in peacefully	Democracy - Voted in peacefully
Degree of Personal Businesses Allowed			
None / Minimal	Moderate	High degree	Very high degree
Any Capitalism?			
None / Minimal	Yes / Moderate	Yes / high degree	Yes / Very high degree
Degree of Personal / Economic freedom			
Government owns most businesses	Yes, but Government nationalizes key businesses/industries & runs them like a business to provide extensive social benefits	Individuals & corporations own almost everything	Individuals & corporations own everything
Any Government Regulations?			
Extensive	High	Moderate	Little to none
Any Personal Taxes?			
Little to none / Government provides what it can	High, unless a country has something to sell like oil	Moderate / Used to build infrastructure (roads, bridges, etc.)	None / Minimal
Any Social Benefits?			
Whatever the government can afford to provide / (healthcare, free education, food programs, etc.)	Yes, extensive (universal healthcare, cost effective education thru college, extensive Unemployment, Social Security, etc.)	Yes, moderate (healthcare for elderly & kids, college if you can afford it, moderate Unemployment, Social Security, Medicare, etc.)	Not many (healthcare if you can afford it, college if you can afford it, no Unemployment, no Social Security, no Medicare)

Still a bit confused about what exactly is modern day socialism? Here's how one high school economics textbook defines it as, "a social and political philosophy based on the belief that democratic means should be used to distribute wealth as evenly as possible throughout a society. Real economic equality can only exist when political equality is coupled with economic equality. Furthermore, economic equality is possible only if the public (meaning government) controls the centers of economic power (key businesses/industries). Also, this type of economic system requires a high degree of central planning to achieve economic equality" (O'Sullivan & Shefffin 35).

In a modern-day socialist country, in order to accomplish their goals of taking care of everyone, including poor people, the government generally votes to nationalize major industries. These include utilities, railroads and, any others like oil. The government then proceeds to operate those industries like a business and uses the profits to help pay for extensive social benefits. In this way it is felt their society can move closer to economic equality.

Of course, each country which is a modern-day socialist country practices socialism a bit different. This is because it is a democratic process. Some countries choose (vote) to have extensive social benefits for people and thus they need to nationalize a number of industries in order to pay for their extensive social benefits. Others choose to have moderate or less benefits and nationalize less industries. Either way, modern day socialists are dedicated to achieving what they can by voting. They have renounced violence, unlike communists. And generally, modern-day socialists believe community comes first, individuals second. Many of the allies we deal with in Europe and other non-European countries fall into this category.

America is somewhat different. Our economic system is a Mixed Modern economy which has elements of a modern-day socialist economy, like a safety net with moderate programs/benefits. In the United States, individuals generally come first, community second. And, because modern-day socialism is voted in by the populace of a country, no one needs to worry any time soon about America becoming a modern-day socialistic country. Just because citizens want to fine-tune healthcare and provide basic healthcare to everyone doesn't mean anyone is going to vote to increase taxes and or nationalize any United States industries soon. America's destiny is not to become a full-blown socialistic country. It just isn't going to happen.

So, relax and let's not shy away from fixing healthcare because some think it will lead to modern-day socialism. Instead, let us begin the process of talking about what might work and how to do it. There is no doubt in my mind that if we can get a group of healthcare professionals, legislators, and some citizens together to study what other countries have done, we will be able to fine-tune our healthcare system and move on with a program that is acceptable to the majority of Americans. After all, according to the United Nations, everyone is entitled to healthcare. Let's reform this needed human right now.

Reform Ideas for Discussion on the Middle Class, Taxes, & the Federal Debt

Everywhere you go today, more and more people in the middle class are losing confidence in government. Why is this?

One reason may be the increasing income gap between the poor, the middle class, and wealthy people. According to Think Progress, "on average, today's upper-income families are almost seven times wealthier than middle-income families, compared to 3.4 times wealthier in 1984" (Salles).

In addition, Inequality.com says, "In the United States, income inequality, or the gap between the rich and everyone else, has been growing markedly, by every major statistical measure, for some thirty years" (Facts Income Inequality in the United States). Worse yet, people in the top 0.1% make over "198 times the income of the bottom ninety percent" (Facts Income Inequality in the United States Gaps in earnings between America's most affluent and the rest of the country continue to grow year after year).

What is it about some wealthy people? What makes them love money so much that they will do whatever they can to make more of it. Perhaps, the Bible passage says it all, when it speaks of how it would be easier for a camel to thread the eye of a needle than for a businessman to enter heaven.

In America, many rich people and corporations, have spent the last 30 years stacking the deck against the middle class. How did they do this? They did it through lobbying efforts and getting people elected to the federal government who were willing to propose and pass tax loopholes that benefited the rich. Essentially, these federal tax loopholes allowed people to keep more of their money. Case in point, it was announced on the news that Amazon earned a profit of 5.6 billion dollars in 2017. Yet they paid zero in federal income taxes that same year (Henney). Meanwhile, middle class families probably paid an average of over $5,000 or more in federal income tax in 2017 because they do not make enough money to qualify for the tax loopholes used by the rich and wealthy corporations. No wonder many middle-class people are frustrated with the government.

In a country that continues to build and maintain infrastructures that benefit businesses, it is mind boggling why many wealthy people try and rig the system to pay as little or no income tax as possible. Remember, even if they do pay, when it is all said and done, they will still be among the wealthiest people in American society. So, why not pay a fair share of income taxes?

On another note, the idea that our founding fathers didn't believe in taxes is a myth. In fact, it was a lack of revenue during the *Articles of Confederation* period that led our founding fathers to create a stronger federal government. When the constitution was written, it included provisions for the federal government to levy taxes so they could build roads, bridges, ports, canals, etc.

Today, many Americans feel taxes are too high. In reality, it's a declining tax revenue since Ronald Reagans' administration, coupled with the fact many of our wealthy people and corporations are often hiding revenue in offshore tax havens, that is the real problem. Add to this the continued deficit spending by the government and you can see why our infrastructure is crumbling.

Ironic isn't it. In a federal democracy taxes are indispensable to facilitating capitalism. Having said all this, below are some important reform ideas on the Middle Class, Taxes, and the Federal Debt for your consideration.

- Having the Line Item Veto power is a necessity for the President of the United States to better manage the federal budget. It is also critical in keeping the government running effectively. If a President has the line item veto, they can veto a specific provision in the budget/appropriations bill, then sign the budget so the rest of the legislation can go into effect. Voila! There may be no government shutdowns, ever again and no pork in the budget.

   And, if Congress really wants the item that was vetoed by the President, it can pass the item in separate legislation with a two-thirds vote to override the President's veto. Checks and balances are so important even today.

- The middle class cannot and should not have to continue shouldering the burden of paying down the debt while the wealthy and global corporations pay little to no income taxes for years.

- The tax table does indeed need to be revised. It is doubtful there is a need to raise the top bracket to ninety percent like in 1960. Such an increase, psychologically on affluent Americans might be a shock. After all, the wealthy are not used to paying such high rates in the modern world. Even some new Representatives in the House believe a top bracket of seventy percent may be a bit too much. What is needed is a commitment like the one from 1945 to 1986 where every President and all political parties were committed to paying down the debt. So, it is true, more revenue is needed.

  For starters, perhaps adding a couple more brackets would be in order with the top bracket being forty-nine percent. This way, affluent Americans will be paying a fair share and will also be able to keep fifty-one percent of their money. Surely, they can live with this in a country that allows them to make as much money as possible.

- When we ask people to pay higher taxes, we need to provide some hope of relief in the future. Perhaps we are in this situation because for years people paid high taxes with no hope of relief in sight.

  Therefore, with a top bracket of forty-nine percent, each year the National Debt declines, in relation to GDP, we should lower the percentage due in the next year. For example, if the National Debt in relation to the GDP declines from say seventy to sixty-eight percent of GDP, then instead of the affluent paying forty-nine percent next year, they should pay forty-seven percent. Surely the tax experts in this country can come up with a tax table schedule everyone can live with that rewards and benefits everyone for helping to pay down the National Debt by paying higher taxes.

- No constitutional amendments for a balanced budget. Forget it, it's a bad idea. Instead, enact a law requiring representatives and senators to be more fiscally responsible by balancing a budget each year until the percentage of debt to GDP is somewhere under twenty percent. That means each year, an amount will be put aside in the annual budget to pay down the debt. Its time has come again, and the FED can help decide on exact percentages and details.

- Only in the event of an economic downturn, like a recession or depression or a declared war, should the federal government be able to revert to a deficit spending budget for the year. In order to do this, the government would have to pass a new law allowing the government to revert to deficit spending to alleviate whatever the challenges are. Note, if you have a Balanced Budget amendment, you cannot do this. The government's hands will be tied because you cannot change anything until you rescind the Balanced Budget amendment. That process often takes years if it gets through the states at all.

- No more **"trickle-down economics"**. History teaches it does not work. No more smoke and mirrors by any party to promote such irresponsible government spending/tax concepts.

- Tax loopholes for the most part should be eliminated. People in the middle class do not make enough money to take advantage of the tax breaks. It is just another way for affluent people and corporations in America to keep more of their money. This is wrong and immoral when we are burdening our children and grandchildren with such a debt. It is wrong and immoral when so many students cannot pay back their student loans in a reasonable time. It is wrong and it is immoral when everyone in America does not have adequate healthcare. Eliminating tax loopholes will go a long way to balancing the annual budget, including setting aside an amount to pay down the debt each year.

- Discretionary Tax Income should be used to **create jobs for the middle class** through the rebuilding of our infrastructures, affordable public education for all students, including the availability of higher education for those who qualify, and for healthcare for every citizen. After that, **a reasonable amount** should go to the military.

Reform Ideas for Discussion on Immigration

To say Immigration is complicated is an understatement. Perhaps, this is why Congress has failed to pass any laws for years to revise the current immigration system. Yet, that is exactly what is needed. Currently, the topic of immigration is tearing America apart. What is happening at our borders is at times, against U.S. law, international law and may be considered crimes against humanity. It's outrageous and cannot be allowed to continue.

Having said all that, let's begin with trying to understand some of the basics of immigration. Then we will summarize some ideas to allow reform to advance.

For starters, people have been coming to North America and the United States as far back as 28,000 years ago during the late Pleistocene period. It was during this time period scientists theorized there was a land bridge between Asia and North America (Crosby 20). People walked across that land bridge and migrated south into North America, Central America and eventually into South America. Then in 1000 A.D., the Vikings came to North America led by Leif Ericsson and some say the Chinese in 1421 (the later hasn't been solidly proven yet but is an interesting theory based on a book titled, 1421 The Year China Discovered America), (The Vikings in Newfoundland). Nevertheless, the big immigrations began in 1492 with the discovery of America by Christopher Columbus and the subsequent years of exploration by numerous western European countries. The Colombian Exchange brought not only goods and services back and forth to Europe and the New World, but people as well (Crosby).

In 1609, a different kind of immigration began in the English colony of Virginia, forced immigration. Africans were brought to Virginia and sold to wealthy landowners as slaves to work on agricultural enterprises as well as to serve as domestic servants. Subsequent years saw slavery continue to expand rapidly into other areas of the thirteen colonies, particularly the southern colonies.

In 1620, the Pilgrims landed in Plymouth Harbor near what is known today as Cape Cod, Massachusetts. That brought about continued migration to the new colonies from Europeans, especially from England. William Penn and his followers arrived in Pennsylvania in 1682. One by one, the thirteen original colonies were founded and by 1750, our founding fathers began to come on the scene. Years later, after the United States was founded and *The Constitution of the United States* was ratified in 1791, people continued to flock to America. With the exception of Africans brought into the United States to become slaves, others came in search of opportunities to live a free and better life for themselves and for their families.

The California Gold Rush, for example, enticed many Chinese to seek their fortunes in the United States. They began arriving in 1848 and often worked as miners, small businessmen, gardeners, domestic servants and in 1865 they began working for the Central Pacific Railroad, helping with the Transcontinental Railroad Project to link it up with the Union Pacific Railroad which was expanding westward. It is estimated that as many as 9,000 to 12,000 Chinese worked for the Central Pacific Railroad. Unfortunately, over 1,000 of them died on the project (Le). The two railroads finally linked up at Promontory, Utah, on May 19th, 1869 (History.com Editors, Transcontinental Railroad).

The next large migration occurred during the 1840's to 1850s. People came from the Ireland area of Great Britain, from various German States, like Prussia (there was no unified second German Empire until 1870) and the Scandinavian countries of Norway, Sweden, Denmark. These immigrants were relatively poor, young and had few skills. And, for the most part they were trying to escape famine, political conflicts and religious persecution in their home countries. They were predominately Christian Catholics (Alperin and Batalova).

Then between 1880 and 1920, more than twenty million people from mostly southern and eastern Europe migrated to the United States. Immigrants came from southern Europe to find better jobs and a better life for their family. Those that came from eastern Europe came for a different reason. They like the Catholics previously mentioned, were fleeing religious persecution (Alperin and Batalova).

After WW II, between 1948 and 1954, many European Jewish people migrated to the United States (Brockman). Estimates range in the thousands, although many also migrated to Palestine in the hopes of creating a Jewish state.

The 1965 Immigration Act resulted in people migrating from parts of the world other than Europe. Beginning in 1970, coming to the United States was the top destination/country for Latin immigrants. And while people from Latin America had always come to America since its founding, now large numbers of Mexicans began coming in the 1990s. Many of the Mexicans worked as domestic servants or migrant agricultural workers. They often worked part of the year and then returned home to Mexico. And, in the last five years, in addition to Mexican migrant workers, large numbers of Central Americans have come from distressed Central American countries (Zhao).

Today the migrations continue, albeit they have slowed from Mexico because of improving economic conditions in Mexico. But now it seems that in the last five years, people are coming in large numbers from distressed Central American countries, like El Salvador, Guatemala, and Honduras (Zhao). Again, it is the same old reasons... they come to seek jobs and a better life for their families. Some come also to escape discrimination and violent persecution from their government and or gangs in their communities. What happens to them when they get to the U.S. southwest borders?

Here is where the road meets the rubber. And right now, the rubber is peeling off like worn tires from a big truck because no extensive reform on immigration has passed in Congress for decades. Here is the situation:

- Many who migrate to the United States, once here, claim asylum.
- U.S. law in 1980 accepted the United Nations definition of asylum. "Asylum is a protection granted to foreign nationals already in the United States, or at the border, who meet the international law definition of a **refugee**." The United Nations 1951

Convention and 1967 Protocol define a refugee as a person who is unable or unwilling to return to his or her home country and cannot obtain protection in that country due to past persecution or a well-founded fear of being persecuted in the future "on account of race, religion, nationality, membership in a particular social group, or political opinion." Congress incorporated this definition into U.S. immigration law in the Refugee Act of 1980 (Asylum in the United States).

- The United States is bound by this definition because the U.S. is a signatory of the 1967 United Nations Protocols and the U.S. Refugee Act of 1980, signed by President Carter.

- Any person who steps foot in the United States without proper papers is in violation of U.S. Immigration Law, unless they apply for asylum. If they do so, it acts as a defense against being deported as soon as possible.

- The process to seek asylum requires much more than simply stating so at the border. A person must fill out an application to declare asylum for themselves and or their family. Here in lies possible problems. If there are language barriers (meaning they are not fluent in English), immigrants may not understand what they are told. Or, border patrol agents may not actually inform immigrants of the process. I suspect to not inform immigrants of the process is in violation of U.S. Immigration Law.

Here is where it gets interesting. Newly arriving immigrants claiming asylum have one year to fill out the asylum application. If they do so, they can remain in the U.S. until their day in court, whereby they must convince a judge that it is imperative for their safety and or the safety of their family they remain in the United States. If granted asylum, they may remain and apply for a green card, which enables them to eventually find gainful employment, pay into social security, pay taxes, and possibly become a U.S. citizen (Asylum in the United States). If they do not complete this asylum application, they are eventually deported.

Now, let's play Nazi Germany 1934. What if they are not told about filling out this essential application or don't understand what the Border Agent is telling them at the time of arrival? Or, they don't fill the application out properly because of language barriers. Or, what if children are separated from their parents at the border and then when their court date comes they have no legal representation because the U.S. does not guarantee them the right to a defense lawyer (Children in Immigration Court: Over ninety-five percent represented by an attorney appear in court). The U.S. Citizenship and Immigration Services (USCIS), a division of the Department of Homeland Security (DHS), can then claim the immigrant(s) are in violation of U.S. Law and therefore must be deported.

Ironic isn't it? The first steps the U.S. takes for people who are fleeing to the U.S. in hopes of a better life...may be an evil, diabolical, immoral act perpetrated on defenseless immigrant(s). Is this what the U.S. has become? Of course not, so one must ask why is this happening and how it is happening? Why are we breaking our own laws and international laws in broad daylight? And, why isn't the justice department doing anything about all this?

Every border agent/manager who lies to migrants when they step one foot into the United States and ask for asylum, knows they are in violation of not only U.S. laws but international laws. Immigrants have every right to do so under our existing laws. In addition, to take children from their parents, to rip babies out of the arms of mothers who are breast feeding them and to put the children and the parents in cages like animals; Well, that very well may be a crime against humanity. A few people have died as a result of this outrageous treatment!

Such crimes should be met with swift justice in the United States and the international community of civilized nations. If there was an independent justice department (one that does not report to or answer directly to the Executive branch) perhaps people would have been indicted. In fact, every border agent/manager who is suspected of violating U.S. Immigration law should be arrested by a U.S. Marshal and charged with violating U.S. and international law. Whether or not they will ever be found guilty is not the point. They should have been arraigned and had their day in court like anyone else in America who violates a law. Anything less is a partial breakdown of our legal system/government laws.

And to the argument, "I was just following orders." Remember, that defense no longer applies. At the Nuremberg Trials after WW II, Nazi leaders were tried for crimes against humanity. Almost to a man, their defense was "I was just following orders." Well, all but a few were found guilty and hung despite that defense. The others went to jail for a very long time.

It is no longer acceptable legally or morally to simply say, "I was just following orders." There is a higher law that prevails. It is the law that Locke spoke of in his writings. It is a law that protects human beings from bestial treatment by governments and individuals.

Furthermore, this country has endorsed the United Nations Declaration of Human Rights and has signed international treaties regarding the migration and immigration of people worldwide. To violate those laws is at the very least, committing a crime in the United States, perhaps even a crime against humanity in the international community.

Perhaps there are many reasons why this is happening now. Some people simply don't believe these things are happening to immigrants. They have been watching politically biased news media shows and simply are ignorant of the facts. Many political talk shows fill people's minds with propaganda, not facts. It is likely they never received all the information on this subject. Or, if they were exposed to the facts, they simply choose not to believe them. They turned a blind eye to what has been reported because of the propaganda currently perpetrated against them. After all, the President himself has said over and over again and the media keeps showing over and over again to the general public, the claim, "the media is the enemy of the people." Repetition is a key characteristic of propaganda. Such repetition of propaganda will result in a percentage of people agreeing with these Nazi/fascist type tactics being used.

It is especially hard to understand those who are white supremacist, white nationalists, or worse, Neo-Nazis. One wonders if these people grew up in America? Or, if they did go to school here, they failed to pay attention in their social studies classes. They failed to see the true history of the United States. They did not understand the labor-intensive efforts of Hispanics and Latino Americans, or African Americans, of Asian Americans, of Jewish Americans, of Hindu Americans, of Muslim Americans, and other minorities, all helping to build America and to influence its culture and ideas. That's a shame because America has always been one of the great melting pots of the world. It is not coincidence that the United States, Great Britain, France and Germany, since WW II have always embraced the concept of a melting pot of incorporated people from different cultures and countries into their own culture to make it better. In the end, they have embraced those enlightenment ideas and it has made their countries the envy of the world. Today, they continue to be some of the top countries people migrate to (Top 25 Destinations of International Migrants).

Despite the challenges with our brothers and sisters who believe the current government immigration policy is good, no one in America should ever have to see headlines or view on TV people being put in cages like animals. Or, people sleeping outside in the open with temperatures dropping into the thirties at night. Or, people being held behind fences with concertina wire (barbed wire) on them like Nazi concentration camps. Or, children separated from their parents at the border. Or, children not able to be reunited with their parents because the government didn't care enough to keep adequate records. Or, newborn babies being breast fed by their mothers taken from their arms and separated by border agents.

Many say America is predominately a Christian nation. If that is true, how can Christians or any other major religion abide such actions? Did Jesus treat children like this? Where is the moral outrage by Christians and other religious Americans? Have we become so morally corrupt that we do not care anymore, even about children? Do Americans really want to live in a country that does this to any kind of people, let alone children? For most, the answer is, "of course not."

The truth is when immigrants place one foot on American soil, they have every right to ask for asylum. And, if they do so, they should receive protection under existing U.S. law and international law.

For those who have kept up with what is happening and reported on it and all those who are fighting this injustice as best they can. People like:

- Mariana Atencio, MSNBC reporter.

- Jacob Soboroff, NBC News and MSNBC reporter (both he and Mariana Atencio have consistently been on the front lines reporting about this crisis).

- Maria Teresa Kumar, President and CEO of the Latino Political Organization, Voto Latino.

- Victoria DeFrancesco Soto, Director of Civic Engagement at The University of Texan as Austin, The LBJ School of Public Affairs.

- Chris Matthews, MSNBC and Rachael Maddow and Lawrence O'Donnell, MSNBC...(apologies for not listing everyone) and more.

We can never thank you enough. God Bless you all for your efforts.

However, for those who like what is currently happening we hope for rehabilitation. Hopefully, there are enough good people left in America to somehow try and bring them back into America's unique culture. Because, if they continue to spew hatred and racism and God forbid, commit hate crimes, they will be hunted down, prosecuted and may go to jail for a very long time.

No one is going to be asked to return to segregation. Nor should they be asked to leave the country if they have lived here for more than ten years and not committed a crime. Furthermore, it is bad enough people have been put in cages and babies torn from their mother's arms, but the majority of the American people will never allow radicals to take control of the United States government. Americans will not go down a deep and dark path where innocent people could be placed more permanently in concentration camps or worse. Don't think it can't happen because it has in other countries. Hopefully, it will never, ever happen here.

The fact America is one of the great Melting Pots of the world is a strength not a weakness. The weaknesses of America lies not in immigration, but in our wealth. We are such a rich country that many Americans don't participate in politics. Many don't even know what is going on. Many have also lost their moral compass, even religious people who support corrupt politicians. Why else would they stand by and allow the government to separate children from their parents? And the rich, well, many are in business trying to rig the system so they can keep more of their money. In fact, some of our wealthiest citizens fail to understand they are rich because of the efforts of labor which many times includes migrant workers in agriculture or the domestic service businesses. Lastly, politicians are too busy today trying to figure out how to win re-election than to have the courage to compromise and begin to fix tough issues like immigration.

Despite all of this, there is hope. We can fix immigration if we get the right people in a room and politicians listen to them and then vote to do what is best for the United States. Do your job Congress. Reform the American Immigration system...now.

Below are some ideas to consider regarding this topic. They are serious starting points.

- Anyone who is not seeking asylum should be educated in their respective countries to go to a U.S. Consulate or Embassy and fill out the proper papers to get on a list for migration to the United States. Furthermore, we should continue to keep prospective immigrants in their respective countries until a proper investigation can be conducted by U.S. officials abroad. If approved, they can then fly to the U.S. with the proper papers and meet with the appropriate border agent to begin immigration status in the U.S.

- If someone is fleeing a war-torn country and or is seeking asylum in the United Stated, they should be treated humanely when they set one foot on American soil. They should be given adequate housing at a temporary border facility (not put in cages) and fed until such time they can meet with an authorized border agent who will explain the process of asylum immigration. They should also be given help, with an appropriate interpreter if necessary, to complete the asylum application process.

- The United States should work with the United Nations over the next few years to develop a system to handle asylum seekers. It is understandable they are fleeing oppression or violence in their own counties or war. But, why can't there be a worldwide system whereby an asylum seeker can go through a process which places them in perhaps, a country that may be more compatible. By this I mean they speak the same language, etc. Such a system would help take the burden off top asylum haven countries like the U.S., the U.K., France, and Germany. Seems like this makes a lot of sense. It would be expensive to do this, but in the long run, the world community could share the burden of relocating migrants.

- Once an immigrant family enters the U.S., no child under the age of 18 should ever be separated from their parent(s) or relatives, nor should they be put into cages, period. Regarding those children who continue to be separated from their parents, the U.S. government should work with the United Nations in coordinating DNA testing. Every effort possible should be made to find the parents of these children.

- All temporary holding facilities should be near a U.S. community. To build them miles from any community is a reminder of what the Nazis did in WW II. Many of the terrible concentration camps, the so-called extermination camps, were built in Poland, outside of Germany because the Nazis did not want Germans to see what was going on at these facilities.

This is not to suggest we are trying to exterminate any group of people or perpetrate horrible atrocities. However, locating these facilities away from American communities does make it easier for private contractors to do things in facilities that may not be appropriate, or illegal, or even crimes against humanity. Case in point, currently in some facilities children are separated from their parents and people are put in cages like animals, sometimes without providing basic human necessities like proper food, water and toiletry articles.

- There are many benefits of building these facilities near American communities. For one, local people could find gainful employment at the holding facility working in responsible jobs. These jobs can include building and maintaining human living conditions like barracks for people to live in until their immigration status is resolved. There would also be jobs maintaining these facilities like maintenance jobs, domestic workers to help with meals for people, etc. People need good jobs in the U.S. and building the temporary holding facilities like a mini city next to an American community would go a long way in providing new immigrants humane services. We should rename these facilities "American Citizenship Integration Facilities."

- If the community does not have a healthcare facility, the government should construct one in the community so that more good jobs will be available to people nearby. By doing this both the community and the newly arriving immigrants will have healthcare nearby, if needed.

- During time in the American Citizenship Integration Facility, immigrants should attend a school each day to learn some basic English, and or some basic American law, etc. Jobs will be provided by or for qualified people in the local community. This is also a perfect place to find out if there are any special needs of the immigrants which the community can help with.

- Once an immigrant seeking asylum gets to the court stage in the process, a public defender should be appointed. And if necessary, an appropriate interpreter for the duration of the court process. Also, since no child is separated from a parent(s), no child should be going through the entire process, especially the court process, without a public defender. No court date should be set until the family has an appropriate public defender, and, if necessary, an interpreter.

- After the court appearance, if asylum status is granted, the immigrants may seek employment in the nearby community or be released to a relative, a church group, or an individual sponsor.

In addition, an Immigration Officer should be assigned to every immigrant regardless of their country of origin. The Immigration Officer will function like a parole officer. Immigrants will be required to keep in touch with them periodically, as well as, over the next seven years, will help guide the immigrant through the citizenship process. Recommendations can be made as to what courses a new immigrant can take to help them learn English. They can recommend credible organizations dedicated to helping immigrants. And, where they can learn more about what the role of an American will be when they become citizens in seven years.

- Note however, if the immigrant(s) are released to a relative, community non-profit group, or an individual, that person, group, or organization must be willing to work with the Immigration Officer in charge of the new immigrant(s) and must accept responsibility for the immigrant(s). This means if the immigrant(s) commit a serious crime, the following should occur... The immigrant(s) should be detained, have their day in court, and if found guilty, deported, period.

- All American Citizenship Integration Facilities should be run by the federal government. The idea of allowing profit-seeking contractors to come into facilities and run them is not working. For one, this should never be a for profit enterprise. This is the first exposure to America new immigrants will have in the United States. Cutting corners to make a profit does not match the goals of the process. It's like education. Often you cannot provide children a good education by running a for profit enterprise. That's a topic for another day. The important thing is that the first impression of the immigrants upon entering the United States should be a good one. Furthermore, once again, having the government run these facilities and provide the kind of goods and services needed will provide jobs to people in the local community. We have to get away from thinking the government can't do anything right. That idea is just smoke and mirrors so profit seeking contractors can make money from this process. The truth is the government does a lot right. They are not perfect, but most people would rather be a government employee making a decent wage with benefits than be an employee of a private contractor who doesn't even provide benefits because they want to make a profit.

- Local communities should be allowed to vote if they want an American Citizenship Integration Facility built near their community. And if they vote no and opt out of the program, they will lose all the federal money and jobs that having a federal facility nearby their community would provide.

- Let's talk Dreamers for a minute. These young people came here with their parents, some of them when they were as young as two or three years old. Dreamers grew up in America, attended American schools, learned English in American schools and in many cases went on to college. In short, America is their country and has been for many years. The reason some of them never became an American citizen is they simply were afraid of being deported to a country where they were not fluent in the language and may never see their friends again.

When you really think about it, children who came here with their parent(s) at any early age did not have a choice. It wasn't their fault. Because of this they did not acquire a green card or go through the appropriate process. We could debate the pluses and minuses, but the bottom line is these kids are culturally American and should be given the opportunity to stay in the U.S. and become American citizens. Also, if their parents have paid taxes all these years and have never been in trouble with the law, they too should be given the option of finally becoming an American citizen or return to their country of origin. To punish people after so many years of living and contributing to communities, seems harsh and not what America is all about.

The government is also at fault. They knew for years that people were coming across the border without proper documentation. In fact, for years the government often turned a blind eye to this because agricultural enterprises needed a source of cheap labor. This brings us to another suggestion for reform.

- If we are not going to prosecute individuals, companies, corporations, and agricultural enterprises for hiring and paying undocumented migrant workers who are here without the proper papers, then we should eliminate the law. Even the current President hired undocumented workers at his hotels and golf courses. What does that say about a country that allows those at the top of society to violate laws without prosecution? If we are not going to eliminate the law, then prosecute all violators.

- Reform Immigration Law now. Stop arguing about it like children and do something, which is much better than doing nothing. And, if your Senators and Representatives continue to do nothing, vote them out as soon as possible.

- In the future, after Immigration Reform, we should strive to follow our laws…all of our laws. If that means someone came here illegally without the proper papers, they need to be deported with due haste. If they return and are captured again, they should be prosecuted and put into jail. This way they cannot keep returning only to be deported again and again. They cannot harm anyone if they are in jail, nor will the U.S. have to incur the expense of returning them to their home country over and over again.

Taxpayers pay a handsome salary each year to members of Congress with benefits and perks like few other people have. Essentially, one of their jobs is to revise laws from time to time. Immigration is one area that needs fixed. In fact, things are so bad, sweeping immigration revisions are needed as soon as possible. No one ever said their job was going to be easy.

Reform Ideas for Discussion on the Executive Branch

The recent abuse of executive power in the modern world is a cause for alarm by all Americans as well as countries in the world which are considered allies. Below are some ideas to increase the checks and balances in the Executive branch and to make it function more in line with a western democratic republican government. These ideas will also help protect the American culture and make it very difficult for a strong man to ever come along and take away the rule of law as well as the human rights and civil liberties all Americans revere.

- The constitution must be changed to state no person is above the law, ever . This means, a sitting United States President can be indicted for a crime and can stand trial while in office.

- If the President is indicted for a crime, within 24 hours of the indictment, the Vice-President shall temporarily assume the duties and responsibilities of President until such time as the President is found not guilty. Whereupon, The President will immediately resume the responsibilities of the office of President.

- If the President is found guilty of a crime in either a U.S. or international court, the President shall immediately resign by virtue of having to serve time for committing a crime. The Vice-President will be sworn in as soon as possible by the Chief Justice of the United States.

- Fine-tune the qualifications required to run for the office of President. This should include having experience in the federal government, having served as a Governor in a State or having served as a mayor of a city with a population of more than one million people. The time has come to stop thinking businessmen or mayors of small cities/towns with no experience on the federal level can do the job of President. Perhaps we should require a presidential candidate to pass an exam like every other professional in America. Would you want a doctor to operate on you or provide you healthcare if they failed the American Medical Exams? The skill set needed to be a successful President is very different than that of a businessman. You need to know about how the government works, American and world history, and basic economics.

- Restrict the Election season/campaigning to 6 months prior to the election. Presidents and members of Congress and the Senate are simply spending too much time and money campaigning. Remember, they are there to work on behalf of the American people. They are not there to enrich themselves by guaranteeing they are reelected.

- The *Emolument's Clause* needs to be revised to reflect the definition of Emoluments with regards to service in the U.S. government. Also, if someone violates the *Emoluments Clause*, then the punishment should be specifically spelled out by law that can be changed from time to time as the need arises. Again, in 1791 there were no Presidents who were CEOs of international businesses. They were elected to serve the people, not to enrich themselves.

- A person who is nominated by their party to run for President and or Vice-President should make available to the Election Commission ten consecutive years of past tax returns with the most immediate one being the previous year to winning the nomination of their party to run for President. These should then be made available online to the public on a website and the media at least sixty days prior to the general election in November. Failure to meet that deadline, should result in that candidate's name being taken off the ballot in all states and territories of the United States of America. And, if people want to vote that candidate in at the general election in November, they are free to do so with a write in vote.

- Any person who fails to attend a Congressional Hearing when asked to do so or to appear before a court of law shall be in violation of U.S. law. As such, that person shall be apprehended and should go to jail for thirty days, just like any other citizen who defies a court order to appear before a judge or grand jury. Upon serving that sentence, if they still refuse to appear before a Congressional Hearing or a court of Law, they shall serve another sentence of six months in jail.

- Furthermore, any President who refuses to allow his staff or a Presidential Advisor or anyone who reports to him from attending a Congressional Hearing or appearing before a court of law, shall also be in violation of U.S. law and temporarily suspended from duties and responsibilities for the same thirty days as the person who is in jail for noncompliance.

Furthermore, the Vice-President shall assume the duties and responsibilities of the Presidency on a temporary basis for thirty days. If the President, upon resuming his/her duties and responsibilities again orders someone to not testify before a Congressional hearing, that President shall be indicted for obstruction of justice and will have to stand trial, like anyone else who violates a law. The Vice-President will again resume the duties and responsibilities of President until such time as the trial is concluded.

- Laws regarding *Executive Directives* also need to be revised. An incoming President **should not be allowed** to overturn a prior *Executive Directive* without the majority consent of Congress.

   This change would provide some stability in running the U.S. Government and in dealing with International Affairs. Failure to do this may result in a catch twenty-two whereby America will be in an endless loop of approving actions, especially international actions, only to disapprove of them when the next administration takes control.

- The President **shall not have the authority** to appoint a temporary assistant manager to a government agency. The President will instead work with the next highest level government civil service member managing the agency until such time as the Senate can confirm the President's choice to become the next agency manager.

- Civil Service members who are qualified, should be considered for cabinet positions.

- Regulations regarding *Executive Orders* issued by the President of the United States should be spelled out in legislative laws passed by Congress in response to changing times.

- Nepotism should be outlawed/eliminated **in all branches of the United States government**, especially the Executive Branch...Period.

- A President should not be able to pardon anyone who is involved in an investigation of a President.

- A President cannot pardon a person serving time in jail for a crime unless the convicted criminal has served a minimum of their sentence and has been recommended to the President for a pardon by the pardon process.

- If a President wishes to have a cabinet member removed, he should ask that person for a letter of resignation. If that member feels they have done nothing wrong and wish to continue working on behalf of the American people, the President should recommend to Congress, based on sound reasons, that Congress should begin impeachment proceedings. If convicted in both houses of Congress by a simple majority, the cabinet head and or high-ranking government official shall be terminated. Otherwise, the cabinet member may remain on the job until their term ends under that President's administration. Remember, cabinet officials are there to help the President serve the American people. They should not be chosen based on loyalty to the President.

Reform Ideas for Discussion on the Electoral College

The Electoral College is obsolete. It has no reason to exist in the modern world where almost every citizen can read and write. Below is an idea to consider which would require a Constitutional change.

- *Article II Section I* of the *United States Constitution* must be changed. The Electoral College should be eliminated for Presidential/Vice-Presidential elections. In its place should be wording that allows for whomever wins the popular vote nationwide, becomes the next President and Vice-President of the United States of America.

Reform Ideas for Discussion on the Judiciary Branch

Once again, we see the influence of radicalized partisan politics having an effect on the integrity of the Judicial branch. And remember, when the constitution was written and ratified there were no political parties. Most likely the founding fathers envisioned members of the judiciary branch deliberating cases on intent or on what was spelled out in the constitution and being a check or balance on the legislature and the president. Founding fathers could not have foreseen what is happening in 2019, with the radical polarization that has even affected the process of selecting judges. Recent political events illustrate this point. These experiences lead most intelligent people to the conclusion the Judiciary branch of government must also be fine-tuned. Here are some thoughts outside the box, on how the process could be improved.

- When there is a vacancy on the U.S. Supreme Court, a committee consisting of one judge from every appellate court of the U.S. Courts of Appeal will provide the President of the United States with three possible competent nominees to fill the Supreme Court vacancy. The FBI will then complete a thorough investigation on all three of the candidates to be completed within six months of the nominations. After that the President will then interview each candidate and select one from the three nominees.

- A hearing must then be conducted by the Senate no later than three months following the President's selection of a nominee. The leader of the Senate cannot delay this hearing as in the past. The hearing will be transparent and made available to the public. The nominee will attend and answer any questions asked of him/her and have an opportunity to defend themselves considering the investigation.

- Following the hearing, the results of the investigation and the hearing will be made available to the public via a government web site.

- Should anyone interfere with this process or tamper with the hearing video/investigation material, including rewriting an abridged version, they will be fined and or put in jail. It's up to Congress to define specific punishments.

- The nominee's name will then be placed on all ballots throughout the United States to be voted on at the next November election. Voters will have the opportunity to confirm the appointment of the nominee to the United States Supreme Court or to reject the nominee's appointment by a simple Yes or No confirmation vote on the ballot.

- If confirmed, the nominee will be sworn in by the Chief Justice of the Supreme Court during a ceremony in December of that year. They will then serve until their premature death, resignation, or mandatory retirement age of eighty.

Reform Ideas for Discussion on the Justice Department

- The President will continue to nominate a competent candidate to become the Attorney General of the United States, heading up the Justice Department, when an opening occurs. Once nominated, a thorough investigation by the FBI will be conducted within six months of the President's nomination.

- A hearing must then be conducted by a joint committee from both the Senate and the House of Representatives no later than one month following the conclusion of the investigation of the nominee by the FBI. The hearing will be transparent and made available to the public. The nominee will attend and answer any questions asked of him or her and have an opportunity to defend themselves.

- Both the Senate and the House of Representatives will then vote to confirm the nominee within one month of the hearing. A simple majority is needed for the nominee to be confirmed.

- Once confirmed, the Attorney General (A.G.), along with the Justice Department, will function **independent** of the President of the United States for a period of eight years or until they are removed from office by Congress. The A.G. will be **a political**. There will be no political lawyering. This is essential if we want our Justice Department to uphold the laws of the land for the people of the United States of America.

- It will be the responsibility of the A.G., with the help of the Justice Department to bring charges against anyone in the United States, including the President while in office or anyone in the government, if they have evidence, he/she violated a U.S. law(s) or international law(s). **No person can be above the law in the United States, including the President and Vice-President**, period.

- The President cannot fire the Attorney General. Government officials are working on behalf of the American people. However, if the President or Congress suspects a government official should be removed from office, including the A.G., the President shall recommend to Congress a hearing should take place to determine if the A.G. or any other high government official has violated a law. The hearing will be held in the House of Representatives with members of the committee being from both the House of Representatives and the Senate. If the conclusion of those in attendance at the hearing is that the government official has engaged in criminal activity, the matter will be referred to the nearest federal court. If the government official has not violated a law but has been negligent in their duties and responsibilities, a trial will begin within 2 weeks in the Senate. Both the House of Representatives and the Senate must vote, within a timely manner, on the removal of said government official. A simple majority vote is all that will be required to remove the government official.

Reform Ideas for Discussion on Women's Rights

There is no question that in today's societies, especially in western cultures, most people believe women should have the same rights as men. This concept goes back again to the enlightenment period and continued in the colonies, especially after founding fathers established the United States of America.

Abigail Smith Adams, first lady of the new United States from 1797 to 1801, was a strong advocate for women's rights. In one of her correspondences with her husband John Adams, while he was serving in the new Continental Congress, she wrote:

Abigail Smith Adams
(1744-1818)

"And by the way, in the New Code of Laws, which I suppose it will be necessary for you to make, I desire you would remember the ladies, and be more generous and favorable to them than your ancestors" (Abigail Adams).

Initially, when John received her correspondence, he thought she was kidding. She was not. Abigail went on to have numerous famous quotes about women's rights.

As a mother of four, she generally stayed behind in Massachusetts to protect their children from the rigors of travel, to raise their children and to take care of the family farm. Because of this she often wrote to John when he was away. A few of her famous quotes from her letters to John regarding women's rights:

- "If we mean to have heroes, statesmen, and philosophers, we should have learned women" (32 Powerful Quotes By Abigail Adams That Reveal Her Mind).

- "Remember all would be tyrants if they could. If particular attention is not paid to the ladies, we are determined to foment a Rebellion, and will not hold ourselves bound by any laws in which we have no voice, or representation" (Abigail Adams).

- "Men of sense in all ages abhor those customs which treat us only as the vessels of your sex" (32 Powerful Quotes By Abigail Adams That Reveal Her Mind).

Just six years after the Constitution of the United States and the *Bill of Rights* were ratified, Isabella Baumfree (known to history as Sojourner Truth) was born in 1797. Unfortunately, she was born into slavery and served several masters in New York before escaping from her master, who often beat her. She was taken in by Isaac and Van Wegenens, who eventually offered to buy Sojourner from her former master for twenty dollars. She remained with the Van Wegenens until the New York Anti-Slavery Law emancipated all slaves in New York in 1827.

From then on, Sojourner worked tirelessly to secure the rest of her children from slavery, including a son still owned by her former master. In fact, she was the first African American woman to sue a white man in an American court. With the help of the Van Wegenens, she was able to win her lawsuit and have her son returned to her (Sojourner Truth).

While living with the Van Wegens, Baumfree became a Christian and in 1843, after a revelation from the Holy Spirit, she took another name, Sojourner Truth. Thereafter she went by Sojourner Truth (Sojourner Truth).

During the American Civil War Sojourner was active in the abolitionist movement in helping to recruit black soldiers for the Union Army. And she worked for the National Freedman's Relief Association collecting food, clothing, and other supplies for black refugees. Following the Civil War, Sojourner became an advocate for women's rights, including the Suffrage Movement (History. Com.Editors, Sojourner Truth). She is best known for a speech she gave during the Women's Convention in Akron, Ohio in 1852. Here is an excerpt from that speech.

Image from the web, freeimages.com

Sojourner Truth
(1797-1883)

"That man over there says that women need to be helped into carriages, and lifted over ditches, and to have the best place everywhere. Nobody ever helps me into carriages, or over mud puddles or gives me any best place! And ain't I a woman? Look at me! Look at my arm! I have ploughed and planted, and gathered into barns, and no man could head me! And ain't I a woman? I could work as much and eat as much as a man - when I could get it - and bear the lash as well! And ain't I a woman? I have borne thirteen children, and seen most all sold off to slavery, and when I cried out with my mother's grief, none but Jesus heard me! And ain't I a woman" (Ain't I A Woman?).

Another African American woman during this same time period, Harriet Tubman was also an advocate for women's rights. She too was a slave prior to the Civil War but escaped north to win her freedom. Tubman was also instrumental in returning to the south numerous times as a conductor for the Underground Railroad, helping other slaves flee to freedom in the north. Estimates vary from seventy to 300 slaves she helped escape to freedom on the Underground Railroad.

During the Civil War, she served as a nurse. In addition, she was recruited to develop a spy ring which helped supply the union army with intelligence on Confederate troop movements, and supply routes. She also helped recruit slaves to serve in the union army. After the war, she became involved in the women's suffrage movement (History.com.Editors, Harriet Tubman).

Image from the Library of Congress

Harriet Tubman
(1822-1913)

Harriet Beecher Stowe was another woman who advocated freeing the slaves and worked in the educational field, especially educating women. She is famous for writing the abolitionist literary work titled, "Uncle Tom's Cabin." She continued to fine-tune her literary skills becoming one of the best writers, not only in America, but in the world.

In 1848, the first convention on women's rights in the United States was held at the Wesleyan Chapel in Seneca Falls, NY. About 300 people attended the two-day meeting.

Elizabeth Cady Stanton, a friend of Stowe, opened the meeting with a fiery speech, as rights for women took center stage:

"We are assembled to protest against a form of government, existing without the consent of the governed—to declare our right to be free as man is free, to be represented in the government which we are taxed to support, to have such disgraceful laws as give man the power to chastise and imprison his wife, to take the wages which she earns, the property which she inherits, and, in case of separation, the children of her love" (History. Com.Editors, Seneca Falls Convention).

Image from the Library of Congress

Harriet Beecher Stowe
(1811-1896)

Essentially, their goals included the right to:
- Vote (suffrage).
- If married, to own property.
- If married, to own their wages.
- A good education equivalent to men.
- Work in professional jobs.
- Divorce an abusive husband.
- Be represented in government.

After the civil war, Stanton hooked up with Susan B. Anthony to "found the National Women's Suffrage Association in 1869. In addition, they created a weekly newspaper titled, *The Revolution* and later co-edited a three-volume publication of *History of Women's Suffrage*" (History.Com.Editors, Susan B. Anthony).

Anthony traveled extensively in the United States giving speeches on women's suffrage. She is also known for voting illegally in the 1872 presidential election. She was arrested and tried and fined $100 for her illegal activity. However, she never paid the fine. Fourteen years after she died, in 1920, the United States government passed *Amendment XIX*, which was ratified on August 18th, 1920, finally, giving women the right to vote. In recognition for her efforts and service to her country, the U.S. Treasury department minted a dollar coin in 1979 with Anthony's portrait on one side. It was the first time a woman's portrait was placed on a U.S. coin" (History.Com. Editors, Susan B. Anthony).

When the Great Depression hit, women faced a new challenge…employment discrimination. Because there were not enough jobs for men, let alone women, married women in many states were not allowed to work. If a young lady was fortunate to have a job before she became engaged, she was forced to quit her job the moment she became married. Women were told in many states that when they married, they had to give up their full-time job.

All of that changed when the Japanese attacked Pearl Harbor on December 7, 1941. As America entered World War II, men were recruited in mass to serve in the armed forces. Eventually, there were over ten million men in uniform fighting worldwide. Because of this there was a labor shortage. There simply were not enough men to work in factories for badly needed war supplies. Thus, women were asked to enter the workforce. Over the next four years a campaign was developed and promoted to get millions of women to work in factories. Many did so gladly to help the war effort. Remember the "Rosie the Riveter" poster? That poster was used in the campaign from 1942 on to encourage women to enter the workforce. There is no question that Rosie was real. It's just that history has blurred the facts on who posed for the picture used on the poster. Three women are credited with being the actual Rosie. All three were photographed while working in military jobs.

Geraldine Hoff Doyle was photographed while working in a naval machine shop in Michigan. Rose Will Monroe was also photographed while working as a riveter at the Willow Run Bomber Factory near Detroit, MI. However, strong evidence points to Naomi Parker Fraley as being the real inspiration for Rosie. One day while working in the machine shop at the Naval Air Station in Alameda, California, Fraley was photographed. In 1942, a Pittsburg artist, J. Howard Miller, developed a poster from the photograph which was used on a poster for Westinghouse Electric Corporation. Later, Norman Rockwell, a famous American artist, developed a cover layout for The Saturday Evening Post showing Rosie in front of an American flag while tramping on a copy of Adolf Hitler's "Mein Kampf (My Struggle)." That issue appeared on May 29, 1943 (History.com editors, "Rosie the Riveter").

Overall, the campaign was a huge success. By the end of the war in 1945, almost all married women, one in four, were contributing toward the war effort by working in factories producing materials and weapons for the U.S. armed forces.

Such new endeavors by women also brought new challenges. In general, women were often under paid what men were making doing the same job. Thus, a new goal was added to the women's rights list...**fair and equitable compensation.**

The 1950s and 1960 also brought new challenges that would forever change the course of women in America. The first was the Civil Rights movement. This was an effort by black people to continue their efforts to assert their human rights and civil liberties in America. Women played a key role in this endeavor.

By 1950, black people everywhere in the United States were struggling to be treated the same as other Americans, particularly in the south. Often they were treated like second class citizens, being denied the right to live in the same areas as white folks. In addition, they were forced to eat in the back rooms of restaurants, and they could not drink out of the same water fountains as other citizens. Also, they were often denied the right to vote in elections and their children could not attend the same public schools or play in the same parks as other children in the community. In order to keep them in line, they were often terrorized,

A mural on an abandoned building in Sacramento, CA - 1946

"Rosie the Riveter"
(1942-)

even killed if they chose to challenge the boundaries of American segregation. It was a social policy that was in opposition to the ideas and words of the founding fathers.

On December 1, 1955, a young lady by the name of Rosa Parks refused to sit in the back of the bus where blacks were supposed to sit. She was a Civil Rights activist, and, on this day, she was perhaps just tired of being treated like a second-class citizen. Her defiance that day provided the spark that launched the Civil Rights movement.

Her refusal to comply with segregation norms began a long, difficult, bloody journey that continues to this day. The journey included many peaceful marches, in which marchers were attacked by dogs and beaten by police and vigilantes. Children on marches were often fired upon by water cannons. Today most of the tactics used then by opponents of civil rights are outlawed in the United States.

Some of the more famous leaders of the Civil Rights movement were assassinated. Even volunteer workers and children were killed in the carnage. Medgar Evers, a World War II veteran, was both an activist and an NAACP field secretary in Mississippi. He was assassinated, shot in the back while in his driveway on June 12, 1963 (Medgar Evers). That same year, on September 15, four girls, Denise McNair, (11), Carole Robinson, (14), Addie Mae Collins, (14), and Cynthia Diane Wesley, (14), were killed while attending the Sixteenth Street Baptist Church, one of the oldest churches in Birmingham, Alabama. Twenty others, many children, were also injured. Bombings were a common tactic used by white supremacists to terrorize black people

Image (Rosa Parks Sitting On A Public Bus)
Freeimages.com

𝓡osa 𝓟arks

(1913-2015)

and those who sided with them in the struggle for Civil Rights. In fact, there were so many bombings in and around Birmingham that the city earned the nickname, "Bombingham" (Birmingham Church Bombing). The following year, in 1964, three young Civil Rights activists were murdered while in Mississippi helping to register black voters. Michael Schwerner, Andrew Goodman (both of whom were white northerners), and James Chaney were murdered by members of the Ku Klux Klan near Meridian, Mississippi (The KKK kills three civil rights activists). Four years later, Dr. Martin Luther King, Jr., one of the key leaders of the Civil Rights movement, was assassinated. While leaving his motel room at the Lorraine Motel in Memphis, Tennessee on the evening of April 4, 1968, he was shot and killed. Dr. King Jr was in Memphis to support a sanitation workers strike (History. Com Editors, Dr. Martin Luther King Jr., is assassinated).

Throughout all this, it was women, like Rosa Parks, Myrlie Evers and Coretta Scott King who picked up the pieces and continued the quest for civil rights. Nine mothers specifically (with the support of their husbands), gave the green light for their children to attend an all-white public high school. On May 17, 1954, the U.S. Supreme Court ruled in *Brown vs. the Board of Education* in Topeka, Kansas that racial segregation in public schools was Unconstitutional (History.com Editors, Brown v. Board of Education). It took a few years but what happened next, took a lot of courage. Elizabeth Eckford's parents decided, along with eight other parents, to allow their children to attend the all-white Little Rock public high school. In fact, it was so controversial, the girls were turned back the first time they attempted to go to school. On the morning of September 4, 1957, Eckford and the other eight students were greeted by a frantic crowd, trying to bar their entrance to the high school. It was not until

President Eisenhower federalized the Arkansas National Guard and sent 1,000 federal troops to Little Rock that the girls were able to attend school on the morning of September 24, 1957. This event became the beginning of efforts to end racial barriers in public education in America (History.com Editors, "Little Rock Nine begin first full day of classes").

(Coretta Scott King at the Democratic National Convention)
Image from the Library of Congress

Coretta Scott King
(1927-2006)

The Civil Rights journey is far from over. America continues to struggle with equality. For example, there are poor schools vs. higher income schools. Different tactics are used today but the result is often the same. However, the courage and efforts of women, as well as men, went a long way in tearing down many of the segregation barriers in America.

Another important milestone for women occurred in 1972. *Title IX of the Education Amendments* banned sex discrimination in schools that year (Timeline for Women's Rights). The result was an immediate increase in athletic programs for girls. Today, girls can play most of the same sports as boys.

The Pregnancy Discrimination Act of 1978 was another milestone for women. It protected pregnant employees and in 1991, the *Family and Medical Leave Act* gave parents the right to be on work leave for a short period of time after the baby was born. This was a step in the right direction but much more is needed in this area.

Problems still continue to exist for parents who take time off, even if they are sick, and then return to work only to find their job has changed. Despite all the legislation over the years, there still are challenges for women earning the same pay as men. For example, in 2009, President Obama signed the *Lilly Ledbetter Fair Pay Act* to reduce/close the Gender Wag Gape. Unfortunately, four years later in 2012, women still only made 77 cents for every dollar a man earned (Alter). This is called the Gender Wage Gap, the total difference between what men earn and what women earn. There are laws on the books that state a woman must be paid the same rate a man earns if they are doing the same job and have the same amount of tenure. But what if a woman takes off to have a baby? Now a male worker, who started employment with a lady, has a bit more time on the job (tenure). And, when it comes to a job opening for a higher position or a promotion, discrimination often plays a role in who gets the better job/promotion. In a "good old boys" company, men are often given the higher paying job/promotion because they have more tenure than a woman who had a baby and is applying for the same job. The result is men make more money than women when you tally up the total amount of money men earn versus women.

Of course, this is not right. Nor is this smart if you are the owner of a company. Whomever is the better candidate for the promotion/management job, should be given that job. Failure to do so is not in the best interest of a business. Nevertheless, old habits die hard.

Sometimes, discrimination has nothing to do with tenure. It is just outright discrimination. A recent lawsuit, filed by the United States Women's Soccer Team, alleges they are being paid less than the men's team and their working conditions are poor. This is a perfect example of economic discrimination (Das). Currently the women are the 2019 World Cup Champions. Their performance is clearly not the issue.

Outright gender discrimination is real, and it affects the Gender Wage Gap. There is no doubt the Gender Wage Gap is much better than it was in the last century. But there is still a long way to go before women are given the same economic opportunities, including pay, that men enjoy.

Since 1776, American women have been fighting for equal rights. This is a fight that is critical if we wish to maintain the political, social and economic culture of America. Whatever Congress, the President, and the nation can do to facilitate equal rights for women should be a top priority. Below are some ideas for consideration and are by no means an exhaustive list. Much more needs to be done in this area.

Ideas for a Discussion on Women's Rights

- **Pass the Equal Rights Amendment for Women.**
- **Paid Family Leave.**
- **Guaranteed job upon return to work following paid family leave.**
- **Prenatal healthcare.**
- **A basic, affordable healthcare plan for all women and their family, taking into consideration special needs as mothers.**
- **The right to not be sexually harassed in any form in America.**
- **When applicable, enforce laws for the right to be the same as a man.**

Ideas for a Discussion on Education Reform

Reforming how students can afford to attend educational facilities is one of the most important things we can do for our country. Young people represent our future. Someday young people will become House of Representative members, Senators, Governors, and local government officials and leaders. The more educated they are, theoretically, the better public servants they will become.

Therefore, we must especially make higher education more affordable for all, not just for the children of wealthy people. Think about it. The way we are going, only children from wealthy families will be able to become our teachers, doctors, etc., in the future. They in turn are going to try and maintain their social status for their families which is exactly the problem we have today.

Education must be affordable for everyone who legitimately qualifies for college. There are ways to do this. Below are some ideas to consider:

- Expand the *GI Bill* to include anyone who gives America two to four years of volunteer service. Volunteer efforts can be in the Peace Corps, Volunteers of America, at hospitals or approved medical facilities, or any other approved volunteer organization helping people.

- The government should set up an optional program for people to have a percentage of their money deducted from their gross pay to later help to pay for their son/daughter to attend college. The government will then invest that money on behalf of the family until such time as it is needed.

- When a student qualifies for college and needs the above funds, the government will release that money to the higher educational organization to help pay for college.

- If a student fails to attend, eighty-five percent of the funds paid into the college fund over the years should be returned to the family. Fifteen percent of the fund should be forfeited to the government to help pay for the expenses of administering the college fund.

- The government should pass a bill making it illegal for financial institutions to loan students' money for higher education that have an interest rate higher than the prime. Also, the terms of a loan used for higher education should have terms that allow for the student to repay the loan off earlier and not pay more than ten to fifteen years after graduation.

- State governments should establish a board of directors for making higher education affordable. The purpose of this organization will be to find ways to reduce the amount a student pays to attend a local college (two-year program). It is very likely between this board and the above call to corporations to help, students would pay very little for a two-year local college program.

- Corporations should be given tax breaks, if they contribute a significant amount of money to a higher education fund for local colleges (two-year programs), trade schools, or technical programs. This money should be used to lower the cost for students to attend those colleges.

- Students should be given reduced costs on their education, if they are willing to work as a student tutor or other available jobs while attending college/university or tech/trade school.

- Loans for Students should also be reduced, prorated or outright forgiven for those graduates who are willing to work publicly as a tutor in a school district, or other educational jobs needed by a local community for a period of at least five years.

- Meal plans should also be available to schools, Monday thru Friday, so that students who come from poor or low-income families or those on welfare, will have at least two good meals a day (breakfast and lunch).

One last item. Don't let anyone tell you we cannot afford to help students with the cost of higher education. The U.S. is one of the wealthiest countries in the world. We are made up of some of the most innovative citizens of any country in the world. If we put our minds to this, ways to help reduce the cost of higher education for students can be found. If we have a negative view and say we can't afford this, then it will be a self-fulfilling prophecy. We won't even look for ways to help reduce the cost of higher education. Also, remember the U.S. spends **700 billion dollars a year on the military budget**. Is that really necessary when we are not at war?

There is no doubt in my mind we can do this. We just need to maintain a positive attitude and begin the process. Because we are Americans, the rest will take care of itself.

Reform Ideas for Discussion on the Right to Vote

A dedication to democracy

Amendment V, Ratified February 3, 1870

"The right of citizens of the United States to vote shall not be denied or abridged by the United States or by any State on account of race, color, or previous condition of servitude" (Constitution of the United States: A Transcription).

We live in a federal democracy. This means that every citizen who wishes to vote should be free to and able to vote. That's how we elect people to represent us in both our federal and state governments. Most of the time today, this happens without a problem. However, that was not always the case. We have a sordid history which at times pointed to states and local governments trying to curtail citizen's voting rights. Below are some important reform ideas to make sure all people who want to vote, can do so.

- Laws need to be strengthened to bring people who obstruct voting in any way to swift justice, including politicians in important positions that can influence voter turnout.

- With the technology we have today, there should be early voting on the internet.

- At polling places there should be a paper ballot in addition to the computer ballot. Also, when the polling places close, a random count should occur between the computer results and the paper ballots on hand. If the results are within one percent difference, the election results are valid. If on the other hand, there is more than a one percent difference, all paper ballots for all candidates should be recounted before a final tally is announced to the public.

- Every registered voter should be able to vote for the candidate of their choice in a primary federal election, regardless of their party affiliation.

- However, if no one wins fifty-one percent of the vote in a primary for their party, then a Runoff election should occur between the top two candidates within that party. If no one in the independent parties receives fifty-one percent of the vote, then they too must have a run-off election. Also, in the run-off election, voters must vote in the party of their registration, except Independents. Independents may vote for anyone from any other party other than a registered Democrat or Republican. The goal of the runoff election will be to have a Democratic candidate, a Republican candidate and an Independent candidate representing all other parties. These three names will then be placed on the general ballot for the next election in November.

- Regarding the upcoming general election...any debates should include the person representing the Democrats, the person representing the Republicans, and the person representing all other Independent parties. People should always have more of a choice than two candidates from the two major parties. The choices should include an Independent candidate representing all other parties.

- Also, if after the general election, no one receives fifty-one percent of the vote there should be a second run-off election held between the two candidates who received the most votes, regardless of their party. This run-off election should be held in 30 days.

- All registered voters, regardless of their party are eligible to vote in the run-off election.

- Whichever ticket (President and Vice-President) **receives the most popular votes** in the run-off election becomes the next President & Vice-President of the United States.

- These same ideas can be adopted for House of Representative elections and for Senatorial elections.
- The Senate should vote on the ideas in *H.R.1*. Trying to reform the election process is better than doing nothing at all.

H.R.1 is a large bill with detailed explanations of how to modernize our election system. Many of the provisions in this bill are worth consideration. For example, in part 1, the bill outlines:

- All states should have internet registration, with online assistance in internet registration.
- All states should also allow early voting via the internet. This would eliminate the need for Sunday voting or having the polls open on more than one occasion.
- Use of the internet to update voter information/ registration.
- Voter protection and security in voter registration/ voting.
- Allow same day voter registration and much, much, more (H.R.1 - For the People Act of 2019). Who would be against the above provisions? Hopefully no one.
- The decision by the U.S. Supreme Court in the Citizens United case was perhaps the worst decision ever made by the court. It is a prime example of how partisan politics may have infiltrated and affected the Judicial branch. Donations to any political person, organization, committee, pact...should be made transparent on a web page with information as to who the donor was and how much they donated to any candidate. Failure to do so is going to destroy democracy in America. What we will end up with is wealthy people buying elections.

- One last item...the federal government should do everything in its power to prevent any foreign government, organization, group of individuals or an individual from hacking into our election voting system for the purpose of interfering in an election to change the outcome. Recent extensive activity by the Russians in the 2016 election and now again in the 2020 election are good cases in point. It is essential to prevent this type of activity in a modern democracy. And, that includes the dissemination of false information on social media sites which is propaganda, meaning it is not true.

Reform ideas for Discussion on Gerrymandering

The radicalization of the two major parties is so pronounced today that it has permeated almost every aspect of American society. Even in the States, the parties try to rig the voting system by gerrymandering districts once they get into power. Gerrymandering is a process by which a political party in power tries to redraw district voting maps in the state legislature so that their party will have an overwhelming advantage in registered voters. Meaning there might be three times the number of registered voters for one party in the district after redrawing the maps. This generally gives that party, the majority party in the new district a tremendous advantage in the general election in November.

In Pennsylvania, Republicans recently tried to do this but the new district voting map was struck down by the Pennsylvania Supreme Court. Sometimes a party gets away with it and sometimes not. Also, Democrats have tried at times to gerrymander district voting maps in the past. In both cases, had it not been for the PA Supreme Court, some of the voting districts would be even more lopsided than they are currently.

This must stop. States need to put an end to gerrymandering by having independent commissions, which are a political, draw up political district voting maps. Furthermore, the courts should continue to be the check and balance against gerrymandering by requiring new maps to be reviewed by the supreme court in that state before going into effect.

Reform Ideas for Discussion on Impeachment

Perhaps, it is time to admit the Impeachment process in the modern world is broken. It is not working as it was intended to function. Historically, there have been four U.S. Presidents whereby the Impeachment process began. Three were impeached. No one has ever been removed from office. So, how did we get to this point?

In 1791, when the U.S. Constitution was ratified, there were few laws and it was hoped that if a President failed to uphold the oath of office and committed misdemeanors and or high crimes, the Congress would begin the Impeachment Process and do what was best for the country. This meant hearings in the House of Representatives followed by a vote to Impeach the President. If the motion carried, the President would be declared Impeached but before he/she could be removed from office, the President would be tried in a political trial in the Senate. At the conclusion of the trial, Senators would get a vote to either allow the President to remain in office or to remove the President from office.

Sounds great doesn't it? So why hasn't' the U.S. been able to bring corrupt leaders to justice like other countries? The answer lies in three words...radical political parties.

You see, in 1791 there were no political parties. It was assumed Congress would do what was the right thing. But times have changed. Today we not only have two main political parties, but they both have become radicalized to the point that it seems their members often do what is best for their party, not the country. The power and the perks of being in power, often far outweigh what is best for America. Today we have tons of laws and if you or I would violate one of those laws, we would most likely have to face justice, perhaps even a trial by jury. Below are some ideas on how to handle Impeachment in the future.

- The Impeachment Clause in the Constitution should be removed from the Constitution.

- Furthermore, wording should be added that **no person is above the law**, including high government officials. If a high government official breaks a law, they should be indicted like any other citizen and given a trial by jury.

- Upon indictment of the President, the Vice-President should assume the duties and responsibilities until the trial is over. After all, what is the point of having a Vice-President if he or she cannot do this.

- Following the trial...if the President is found not guilty, he or she would once again resume the duties and responsibilities of the office. On the other hand, if the President is found guilty, the Vice-President would be immediately sworn in as the next President by the Chief Justice of the U.S. Supreme Court. Such action would clear the way for the guilty President to leave office and begin serving the sentence handed down.

Reform Ideas for Discussion on The International Criminal Court (ICC)

If we ventured on to the streets of any small town in the U.S. or even a large metropolitan area and asked, "what is the ICC?," how many people do you think could answer that question? Probably not even two out of ten people would know the answer. Too bad because they should know it.

Following World War II, the ICC was developed in response to atrocities, war crimes, crimes against humanity, and unprovoked aggression by one country against another. You would think the world and humanity learned its lesson after the atrocities and crimes against humanity committed by the Nazis and the Japanese during WW II. Apparently not...

Fortunately, a group of international diplomats got together and decided there should be a permanent international court to punish these types of crimes, since the country the perpetrators are living in, almost always has trouble prosecuting their citizens for crimes against humanity. Thus, an international treaty (The Rome Treaty) was written in 1998. That treaty established the International Criminal Court (ICC) in the city of The Hague in the Netherlands. Its purpose is to bring people to justice via an international tribunal for war crimes, atrocities, crimes against humanity, and genocide.

That means arrest warrants will now be issued, and perpetrators of these type of crimes against humanity will be hunted down, even if it takes years. Once captured, the perpetrators would be extradited to The Hague where they will stand trial. If found guilty, they could spend the rest of their life in prison. The ICC does not believe in capital punishment.

Most nations in the world have ratified the treaty that established the ICC. Unfortunately, the United States has not fully ratified this treaty.

It is really very simple. If Americans feel the world should not punish our leaders when they break international laws, then we cannot hold ourselves to standards of being this incredible world leading country that others should respect. As many mothers across America have said many times when their children were growing up. "You can't have your cake and eat it too." Below are ideas on what to do about this dilemma.

- The U.S. is an incredible country, promoting all the human and civil rights in social and political traditions mentioned in this publication. Therefore, the U.S. should ratify the Rome Treaty, and the U.S. should become a full-fledged member of the ICC.

- In the future, when a U.S. leader or a member of the military steps out of line and are not punished by the United States, the ICC will issue a warrant for their arrest. The U.S. will then extradite them to the Hague for a fair trial. If found guilty, they will receive a punishment **the world sees fit**. People throughout the world will respect America more if we join the ICC than if we sit on the sidelines and do little or nothing at all.

Reform Ideas for Discussion on the Military

Since World War II, the United States has continued to spend an incredible amount of money on the military and has become involved in numerous regional conflicts all over the globe. Today, despite the fact the United States of America has the best trained military and the best military hardware of any nation on earth, the government continues to spend more each year than all the other countries of the world added together. The 2019 U.S. Budget for the military was estimated at $869.5 billion (average from Amadeo/Mil). The next largest competitor was China. Their estimated 2019 military budget was $177.5 billion (Mil).

Why does America continue to spend such outrageous amounts on the military. We all agree we need to be ready at all times to protect the United States in the event of attack. But, if there are no conflicts, cutting back on the military budget could help in other areas. Money could go toward helping students reduce their college costs. It could go to helping reduce healthcare costs for everyone in America. It could be used to fix our infrastructures and so much more. Who knows, maybe we can even build high speed rail lines and modernize our ports. Seriously, we need to take another hard look at reducing military spending. Below are some ideas to do just that.

- A commission should be established to see how military expenditures can be reduced.

- When regional conflicts arise in the world, we should strive to work through the United Nations as has sometimes been done in the past. In this manner, there would be other countries providing soldiers and equipment as well as the United States. This would reduce the amount needed to be paid to help others during foreign conflicts.

- As a guideline, annual budget expenditures on the military should generally not exceed 150% more than the next country in the world with the highest spending amount on their military. For example, if China is spending $215 billion on their military budget next year, we should not spend more than $322 billion in our budget next year.

- Any product manufactured outside of the United States for the military, or better yet, for anything, must adhere to the same requirements as if the factory was in the United States. That means employees are paid a minimum hourly wage, OSHA standards apply in the workplace, environmental standards apply, and quality standards must also apply.

Reform Ideas for Discussion on the Second Amendment

Another tough one...discussions on the second amendment can get heated. Yet, something clearly needs to be done. Too many people are losing their life by gunshots, especially in metropolitan areas. That includes weaponless people being shot by police.

The statistics on gun deaths in this country are staggering. Last year almost 40,000 people died from gunshot wounds. That is the highest number in nearly four decades (Howard). That's more than the estimated number of people who die in car accidents each year, about 32,850 people (Car Accident Statistics in the U.S.).

Clearly, we have a problem in this country when it comes to guns. Our children now have to be trained on what to do when an intruder, possibly with a gun, enters a school building. They are currently taught to either run to safety or lock themselves in a school room and pray the shooter can't get in. Think about all this and how outrageous it is that children must be afraid of gun violence in schools. Is there no place safe in America? Something needs to be done soon. Below are a few ideas to think about.

- Background Check reform...make the background checks extensive, including looking into whether a person has current mental issues. In Australia, background checks sometimes take thirty days to complete. Why can't we make background checks also extensive in the United States?

- Curtail gun shows. Do not allow anyone to sell a gun to a person and allow that person to leave the gun show with the gun. The paperwork can be started for the background checks at the gun show. In addition, if the seller wants to sell that firearm, they should be affiliated with a licensed gun dealer. There is no reason why they cannot work out an agreement to share the commission on the gun if a green light is given once the background check is complete. The sold gun can then be either shipped or held for someone to pick it up at the licensed gun shop. Again, only licensed gun shop owners should be selling guns directly to the public.

- Ban military assault rifles/pistols. Ordinary citizens have no business owning these types of weapons.

- Ban mega cartridges, which have more than eight bullets in them. Ordinary citizens do not need to have mega cartridges.

- Allow people to continue owning shotguns, pistols with smaller cartridges and hunting rifles for deer and other game animals.

- Too many unarmed people are being shot by police. This is not to say the police should not defend themselves when on duty or in the act of performing duties. On the contrary, it is to say this is an area where reform is desperately needed as soon as possible. One possibility is to think about adding an accidental shooting law, much the same way people are charged with involuntary manslaughter following a vehicular accident that results in loss of life. If someone dies as a result of proven negligence , the person who accidentally killed another human being should be and must be held accountable in some way.

- If your House of Representatives member or your Senator refuses to compromise on gun safety, then it's time for you to think about voting someone into office who is more in line with your thinking on this subject, regardless of their political party affiliation.

Reform Ideas for Discussion on Welfare

This too is a tough subject. There have always been poor people in a society. And no matter what is done, the truth is there may always be poor people. However, what is disconcerting is the number of people dropping below the poverty line. The federal poverty line is "a measure of income used by the U.S. government to determine who is eligible for subsidies, programs, and benefits" (Amadeo). This measure changes from year to year based on inflation. Below is a chart showing the current poverty lines based on family size.

Number of People	Total Income for Residents:		
Household	48 States & D.C.	Alaska	Hawaii
1	$12,490	$15,600	$14,380
2	$16,910	$21,130	$19,460
3	$21,330	$26,660	$24,540
4	$25,750	$32,190	$29,620
5	$30,170	$37,720	$34,700
6	$34,590	$43,250	$39,780
7	$39,010	$48,780	$44,860
8	$43,430	$54,310	$49,940
9+	$4,420	$5,530	$5,080

Added for each person
(Annual Update of the HHS Poverty Guidelines)

In 2000 there were about 31.58 million people living below the Poverty Line in the U.S. That number increased during the "Great Recession" to 39.83 million people in 2008. And, by 2014, it rose again to 46.66 million people living below the Poverty Line. Since then the efforts of both President Obama and President Trump have reduced the number to 38.15 million (Duffin).

Clearly, these kind of numbers of people living below the Poverty Line create a tremendous burden on the U.S. welfare system. The average number of people who needed assistance from the government just to put food on the table and to survive in the past eight years is about 44.31 million people. That's a staggering number. And, a lot of tax dollars both from the Federal and State governments go into helping people put food on their tables to feed their families. Below are some ideas to ponder on how to reform the welfare system in America.

- There is no reason why people on Welfare could not be sent out into the community each day/week to help with community projects. The local welfare office could coordinate a work schedule for welfare recipients with local governments and the local community. The work projects could range anywhere from painting local kids' playgrounds, painting public maintenance buildings, maintenance work in public parks, crosswalk attendants for schools, library help, etc. Also, if nothing is available to do on a given day, recipients should report to an unemployment office where they can be retrained to re-enter the work force.

- In return for their efforts, each week, welfare recipients would receive a check on Friday for the work performed during the week. Note, if they only showed up for work on three days, then they will get paid for three days.

- In addition, recipients should receive a coupon booklet

every two weeks which would help purchase good, nutritious food at the local grocery store. These coupon booklets would be similar to the ones handed out during World War II. The food stamps would include stamps for necessities like milk, bread, meat, vegetables. Welfare recipients would no longer be able to use food stamp coupons to buy junk food like soda, chips, and other processed foods unless they used the money received from working. A poor diet is the biggest contributor to health problems for people with low incomes. Therefore, people should be encouraged to eat healthy. Eating too much junk food only leads to medical issues and increased healthcare costs.

- One last thought...openings for government info-structure jobs...like fixing roads, building port facilities, fixing bridges, etc., are great opportunities to get people off the unemployment and welfare rolls. Applicants for such jobs should receive preferential hiring in an effort to help people find more stable jobs. Working as a laborer and possibly getting trained on construction equipment may very well lead to regular employment for people in the future with a private company doing similar work.

Reform Ideas for Discussion on Climate Control and the Environment

Much has been discussed about how to sustain our unique American culture. Discussions have included examining a historical background of where precious U.S. human rights and civil liberties came from and where they are in our important political documents. In addition, we looked at some social history and its importance in our culture. Also, we put forth some important reform ideas, both for our constitution and for changing various laws. In addition, we reviewed some basic economics and reflected on important reform ideas about taxes, deficit spending and the federal debt. However, there is one more area we need to address, which in the long run, is equally as important. In fact, it probably should have been first on the list. This area is climate control and the environment.

What is gained if we succeed in passing needed reforms but are unable to sustain the environment for future generations? What is gained if the oceans continue to rise and major land areas are inundated with water? What is gained if future generations need to wear masks to breath when they go outside? What is gained if future generations are unable to eat the kind of nutritious food available today because it is almost impossible to grow natural crops anymore? And, what is gained if our oceans, bays, and rivers are so full of dead zones they cannot host life?

The truth is, all of this will be for nothing if the only planet we know as our home is destroyed. God gave us this magnificent world and it is up to us to take care of it. If this was a high school class, we would probably have earned a "D" grade at this point on this subject.

Sustainability includes the environment. It is also the ability to meet today's wants and needs without limiting the ability of future generations to meet their wants and needs. At this point, there may not be enough left for future generations to meet their wants and needs. Furthermore, this is not something the United States can do alone. We must work together with other world leaders in both the political and science sectors to solve global environmental issues.

Some of these issues involve addressing environmental damage, rapid population growth, international conflicts, and a growing number of people who currently live in poverty. Each day, we turn on media devices to see yet another story of environmental degradation. In *Illustration 1.1, Sea Ice Extent from the National Snow and Ice Data Center*, we see how much the polar ice cap has melted since 1979. And while we can argue until the sun comes up about what caused this, the immediate problem is the reality of rising oceans. Again, if we do not start to plan for this now with others, large parts of current land masses, world-wide, will be under water and unusable by the end of the century.

Illustration 1.1. Sea Ice Extent from the National Snow and Ice Data Center

In addition, more renewable green energies need to be developed in order to sustain a standard of living for future generations. These energies include developing wind, solar, biodiesel, hydro, and geo-thermal energy (Hibbard, M.P.A., Wheeler, M. ED, and Church, 7). We have the potential to do this. For example, the mid-west is a perfect place for wind energy and our southwest is a perfect place for solar farms. However, all of this is going to be expensive. It is imperative the government is involved. It cannot all be done in one year. It may take twenty to fifty years to do it right. Who knows, it may take 100 years.

Another two areas that need attention are the rapid population growth in the world and the number of people who are living in poverty. The U.N. is working on some goals to try and address poverty, but all nations, especially the United States needs to participate if these issues are to be solved.

In 2020, the "pin code" of the world is 1114. A population pin code means there are:

1 billion people living in the Americas,
1 billion living in Europe,
1 billion living in Africa, and
4 billion people living in Asia.

If you add all of this up there are about seven billion people living on Earth. By the end of the century, it is estimated the pin code of the world will be 1145. That's eleven billion people (Rosling)! Future growth is expected to occur in Africa (three billion more people) and Asia (one billion people more) (Rosling).

The challenge is how to bring Africa's standard of living close to that of people living in more developed countries, like the United States, western Europe, or Australia.

Believe it or not, everything ties together. By that I mean we can reduce population growth by people having better access to health care and family planning, by young people earning higher levels of education, with improved rights for women, and increased economic opportunity. For example, by improving the rights of women in particular, not only in the U.S. but all over the globe, educated women will marry later, have fewer children, will be more likely to send their children to school, and tend to earn more money to support their families (Hibbard, 11).

The risk of withdrawing from the world stage and not helping to resolve global issues could result in increased international conflict. Poor people in the world are not going to stand by forever while the United States and western Europe live like kings. To understand this better let's examine the ecological footprint of people living in India, the United States, and on average, the world.

Ecological footprint is a measure of the land area, lakes and rivers, seas, and resources and infrastructures necessary to support a person (Hibbard, 16). The stats for the average ecological footprint of people living in India is roughly two acres. In the United States it is 23.6 acres. The average ecological space on Earth per person is 4.7 acres (Hibbard, 16). Clearly, developed countries like the U.S. are consuming too much when compared to the rest of the world.

All this is great if you live in the United States. But what if you are currently one of those three billion people estimated to be living in extreme poverty somewhere in the world? In 2013 it was estimated almost half the world lives on $2.50 per day (Shah). Is it fair for some to consume so much while others have so little? The truth is, if we do not reduce our ecological footprint, while at the same time helping to raise up three billion people out of poverty, there will be future conflicts over water, food, and other world resources. Is there anyone who wants their children to die in such conflicts?

Having said that, we have a wonderful opportunity staring at us. We can help sustain not only America's political, social and economic culture by making the needed reforms suggested herein. We can also help raise the standard of living for poor people all over the world. If we do this we can develop and provide jobs and business for U.S. citizens. How about that…instead of jobs moving overseas, factories will be busy here, making replacement parts for equipment shipped overseas to farmers or local governments to provide water resources, and help grow agricultural products more efficiently. All that is needed is the government to provide the incentives for businesses to help others overseas. It's kind of like the *Marshall Plan* years ago when the U.S. helped rebuild Europe after WW II. At that time, there was a great concern that the U.S. economy would lapse into a depression again after the war. But, it didn't because U.S. factories were kept busy and people kept working to rebuild Europe and Japan. And, instead of them being enemies after the war, they became America's friends and allies.

So, what will we choose? Will it be reform, or will it be chaos and perhaps even war in the future? Will we look to the future or to the past? The choice is ours to make.

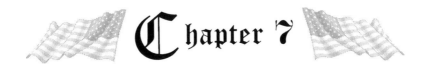

Chapter 7

A Call to Reform

To be an American means many things but it begins with embracing the human rights and civil liberties noted in this book. And because Americans embrace these important human rights and civil liberties, it also means you will respect a person for being who they are regardless of their gender, color, religion, language, ethnicity or sexual preference. It means you believe in religious toleration, allowing others to worship as they please and not forcing a particular religion on other adults or on children in school. It means you are dedicated to democracy and the rule of law. It means you believe in promoting the middle class, yet allowing people the freedom to acquire wealth, provided they pay their fair share of taxes. It means you want to help the less fortunate, provided they work to become middle class citizens. It means you are against discrimination in all forms, especially against women. Hopefully, it also means you want to help sustain our unique historical, political, social and economic culture through continual reforms to make the government work for everyone. Top on the list are reforms designed to provide jobs, healthcare, and a good education for all Americans.

Being an American means there is always a lot of work to do. We won't always agree on everything, but we need to begin now to fine-tune and sustain our unique American culture.

Who will stand with us to meet these challenges? Who will stand with us to make America, as former President

Ronald Reagan once spoke of as being, a "shining city on the hill."

We can be that city again, but we must begin the reform process now so our allies and other countries around the world will once again trust us. We must begin this process now so that once again our government will be able to provide the goods and services our citizens need and want. We must begin the process now so that we can modernize our infrastructures. We must begin now to ensure we will continue to be the leader of technology in the world. We must begin this process now to reaffirm and uphold our founding fathers' beliefs in human rights and civil liberties. In so doing, we can guarantee no person of power/government will ever take away those precious, important human rights and civil liberties either now or in the future. And we must begin now to try and minimize partisan politics so that our democracy can survive and thrive effectively, both now and in the future.

We throw the gauntlet down in front of you. Many have lost faith in the federal government of the United States. But we cannot accomplish goals and objectives without the help of our government. Therefore, we need to prioritize reforms and we need to begin now to implement these needed reforms. No more, "Oh, that'll never happen." As Americans, we have dared to change our government three times already. The first was the Continental Congress during the Revolutionary War. The second was the *Articles of Confederation*. The third was the *Constitution of the United States*. Since then, we have been able to make periodic changes through amendments and laws. Luckily, our founding fathers gave us the chance to make changes to our government without having to pick up guns and fight a civil war for change like in 1776 and in so many other places in the world today. If people set their minds to it, changes can be made without violence or civil war.

So, will you pick up the gauntlet and help? Will you join the fight to make our unique American culture sustainable and our government less partisan and more effective? If so, visit us. Our website is:

www. *ACallToReform* .com

Once there you will be able to register and join with others who care about reforming the government of the United States. In addition, you can visit an online forum where you can discuss specific ideas freely with others. Think of these chat rooms as enlightenment salons of old. During the Enlightenment, people were often invited to attend a session at a salon where they could hear someone discuss ideas on how to reform society and the government. After the presentation, they most likely spent hours socially discussing reform ideas. Of course, wine was served then but since our forums are electronic, you will have to forego the wine, unless you choose to have a glass at home while participating in a discussion.

From the chat sessions we hope to develop a fine-tuned worded document that prioritizes reform ideas. This document can then be ratified by registered delegates at a future conference to be determined at a later date. If the document is ratified at that conference, it will be presented to every Senator and Congressman/woman in the United States government. At that time, we will call upon Congress to either call for a constitutional convention or to enact these needed reforms as soon as possible!

Thank you for purchasing this book and taking the time to read it. Please don't let it end here. Get involved by visiting our website soon!

Epilogue

As this book is being prepared for publication, the COVID-19 Coronavirus is raging throughout the world and spreading across America. This one event, more than any other since World War II, emphasizes the need for reform in an effort to modernize America's federal government.

As everyone knows, the world is much different today than in 1791, or one-hundred or even fifty years ago. There is an extensive interconnection thru businesses and technology with other cultures and countries around the globe. Even if Americans wanted to become an isolated country again, it would be next to impossible. Businesses, for example, operate in multiple countries making various products for use by global citizens. According to some estimates, thousands of U.S. factories have been moved overseas the last twenty years. Because of this, businesses leaders travel daily to all parts of the globe. In addition, people travel to seek tourist destinations for many purposes. There are destination weddings as well as people traveling to party destinations during college breaks. People also travel to unique historical and cultural sites on vacations and much more. As a result, most governments not only worry about citizens entering an unfriendly political environment, but also being exposed to a possible natural disaster or a communicable disease. Worse yet, if it turns out the disease is a pandemic, (a disease that spreads to multiple continents and infects a large number of people in multiple countries), governments may not have the expertise or the resources to handle it properly. Unfortunately, this means when citizens return home, they could be infected with the disease.

Scientists and politicians after World War II foresaw such a scenario. This was one of the main reasons they established the World Health Organization (WHO). It was hoped the WHO would help minimize a communicable disease or a pandemic no matter where it began or where it spread throughout the world. This is not to say the WHO can definitively control such events. It's certainly not a perfect organization but the purpose of it is well founded, especially in a world where the environment is becoming more and more unfriendly to people every year. However, it is difficult for the WHO to help nations if government leaders are not willing to work with them. Take for example the current administration in America. When the WHO developed a test for the spreading coronavirus to be used in less wealthy countries, why didn't the current U.S. administration request the test to see if it could be used effectively in America? Where is the logic in this? A much wiser decision would have been to take the test and use it until American scientists and medical researchers developed a better one.

Unfortunately, it would appear initially, the leadership in America was ill prepared for this pandemic. Each day the media talks about this program and that program being either diminished or eliminated at the federal level because the current administration did not see the need for it. In light of the coronavirus, COVID-19 pandemic, one has to wonder how government leaders were so short-sighted?

Perhaps the answer to this question and others goes back to the topic of qualifications. In *Article II, Section 1* of *The Constitution of the United States* the qualifications to become President of the United States are as follows:

"No Person except a natural born citizen, or a Citizen of the United States, at the time of the Adoption of this Constitution, shall be eligible To the office of President; neither shall any Person be eligible to that Office who shall not have attained to the Age of thirty-five Years, and Been fourteen Years a Resident within the United States" (The Constitution of the United States: A Transcription).

Think about this for a minute. The current President of the United States was not a previous member of either the federal House of Representatives, nor the Senate. He was also not a former Governor of a state. Nor was he an Assistant Governor of a state. In addition, he was not even a member of a state legislative body. Nor was he even the mayor of a major city. In fact, he wasn't even the mayor of Shiremanstown, PA (a small town on the west side of the Susquehanna River about six miles from the capitol of Harrisburg). Yes, he was a business leader. However, the skill set to manage a family business is much different than the skill set needed to be President of the United States. Because he never had any executive experience in either Congress or managing a state, he also had little experience with the various federal government agencies, why they exist and how they work.

At this point, you might say, "he had experienced people surrounding him." Maybe, maybe not. If a leader of any country surrounds themselves with yes people or political cronies, then they too do not have any experience in running a government. For example, why was the current Secretary of Education put into that cabinet position when she had little to no experience in that field? In fact, she never attended a public high school. Her children did not attend a public high school. She never served as a teacher nor did she have any post college degrees in education.

And, what about the philosophy of a modern-day political party? Here is where the discussion of radical polarization comes into play. What if the party elite who is in charge, believe like they did in 1929, there is no need for an expanded federal government role?

President Herbert Hoover, in 1929, believed less government was better. He too was a businessman. When the Great Depression began, he called numerous industry leaders and spoke to them about doing whatever was necessary to keep people employed. He begged them, if need be, to cut worker wages but not to lay people off. As a result, business leaders nodded their heads yes, but in the end, they did what they needed to do to keep their firms afloat. They laid off numerous workers.

When President Franklin D. Roosevelt was elected in 1932, he didn't ask for cooperation. He was a former governor of New York and knew he had to take the bull by the horns so to speak and lead. He passed safety net legislation and tried to create jobs for people. During this time period, the Tennessee Valley Water Authority was established as well as the Hoover Dam was built. He also created conversation corps to help put money into the hands of working people who were willing to help build state parks, and more. Fortunately for Americans, President Roosevelt did not care about labels like "Socialism." He cared about working with all members of Congress to help working Americans, or we should say, unemployed Americans.

This past week, Congress drafted with the help of many people including administration officials, a $2.5 billion coronavirus survival bill to help people and business during this time of crisis. It passed unanimously in the U.S. Senate. It also passed overwhelmingly in the House of Representatives. In fact, many members of the House of Representatives returned to Washington D.C. at their own risk, just to sign the bill (another area of reform needed… at times like this, why couldn't they have used technology to cast their vote from home?). At any rate, they did pass the bill and that's the good news.

The bad news is when the President signed this critical piece of legislation, which by the way isn't perfect as it was a compromise bill in numerous areas, not one member of Congress from the opposition party was present. It really doesn't matter much whether or not opposition leaders were not invited to the signing or if they chose not to attend. What matters is it illustrates the infestation of radical partisan politics, especially in the current administration. No good for the nation can come from such a political reality.

The truth is many Americans from both major political parties worked to mold that piece of legislation. As such, representative from all the groups that helped make this a success in an era of radical partisanship, should have been invited to attend the signing of the bill. It would have been a signal to all citizens that in a time of crisis, Americans can put away their political differences and do what is best for the country. Sadly, this did not happen.

At times like this, America needs national and state leaders with the right qualifications. Leaders who can put themselves above party politics for the good of the nation. America especially needs a President who understands the role the national government plays in managing not only the economy but also managing natural disasters and or pandemics. That role is often to take the lead in assisting states to do what they are not capable of doing alone. In the case of a pandemic, you are at war with a disease, which if not effectively managed, will kill many citizens. Most states are unable to handle such an event on their own. The federal government must take the lead in coordinating and if necessary, providing needed medical supplies and equipment to states. It must also coordinate the efficient use of those supplies and may need to provide funds to state governments in an effort to help people weather the storm.

Herein lies the beauty of Federalism. The founding fathers established this type of government because they understood both the need for states to have freedom and a say in providing citizens with needed services, as well as the need for a strong central government to protect life, liberty, the pursuit of happiness, human rights and civil liberties for all citizens in America. In addition, a strong central government has the advantage of being able to take the lead in helping states provide all citizens with a strong safety net and with needed services during times of extreme danger.

Case in point, is the current pandemic. Each day citizens watch the media and learn that the virus in many areas is progressing faster than states can provide medical care and services to handle it. This is a perfect situation for the federal government to take the lead in helping states. In fact, the Defense Production Act, passed in 1950 and reauthorized over numerous times, was designed to do just that. It can allow the federal government to become involved in matters such as minimizing price gouging by individuals and businesses for the sale of equipment during a time of extreme danger. In addition, the federal government can prevent destructive competition among states for supplies and only the federal government has the power and ability to effectively coordinate the manufacturing/requisitioning of needed supplies (providing important factories are still located in America). So, as of this date, why hasn't the current administration fully invoked the Defense Production Act to help fight the coronavirus covid-19 pandemic?

Perhaps looking back, the current administration should have left the National Security Council's (NSC) Pandemic Response Unit intact. They may have initially been able to encourage the President to take a more aggressive approach in fighting the pandemic. The President said he did not know anything about it being defunded and personnel laid off. Yet, he approved the budget cuts that did just that.

It has also been said the NSC's Pandemic Response Unit had developed a pandemic playbook so to speak. Yet, the current administration did not feel it was important enough or did not believe in science enough to follow that playbook once the coronavirus came to America's shores. Since the Pandemic Response Unit was dismembered, we may never know what was actually in that playbook. But, for discussion purposes, suppose there were response stages established for the federal government to follow. How would it have made the government's response different? Below are some ideas of what could be done in the future if we have a play booklet at the outset of a pandemic.

Pandemic (P) Stage One:
The Pandemic spreads to multiple continents,including the United States with thousands sick and hundreds dying. Appropriate government agencies like the CDC (U.S. Center for Disease Control) are working with WHO to try and contain the sickness. Also, CDC agents are sent to the epicenter of the pandemic to try and learn as much about it as possible. Everything is coordinated with the WHO by the CDC.

Pandemic (P) Stage Two:
Containment is failing. The President invokes war time powers to ramp up the production of medical/hospital supplies. This means there must be factories in the United States that can retool their operations to produce these needed supplies. Never again can we allow factories in this important industry category to establish primary bases of operation overseas without having a large base of operation in the United States. Also, during this stage, military doctors/ nurses and last year medical students should be trained to work with diseased citizens.

Pandemic (P) Stage Three:
Schools and Universities are closed. The military begins to set up additional triage centers in universities and if need be, high schools, to handle the growing number of patients and the overflow from hospitals. Most universities have laboratories nearby which could be of help to these centers. It is essential at this phase there be coordination by the states and the federal government to handle the manufacturing and the delivery of needed supplies/equipment. States can handle the coordinate the overflow of patients.

Pandemic (P) Stage Four:
All non-essential businesses are closed. In addition, people are ordered to stay home. The only exceptions to this is for people to go to the grocery store, doctor's office, etc. Also, the national government reaches out to people and to state governments to try and help people survive the quarantine period. This means financial help to states for unemployment and perhaps even the passage of laws prohibiting foreclosures on houses for lack of a mortgage payment. Perhaps, mortgage payments could even be forgiven during this time of crisis. Remember, business will come back but only if people survive. The safety and health of people must be paramount.

Pandemic (P) Stage Five:
When we have a certain time frame, based on the disease, without any future cases, businesses can resume operations and children can go back to school. At this time, because no one state can do it all alone, the federal government, in coordination with state governments, can decide how to best help businesses get back to normal.

Pandemic (P) Stage Six:
Pray the disease does not come roaring back. If it does, repeat the previous stages.

Of course, these ideas are an example of Monday morning quarterbacking. But, if the right people, not political cronies but experts in their field get together, they will be able to come up with an intelligent plan to deal with future diseases and or pandemics. Note, this will only happen if we modernize our federal government and minimize the radical partisan politics. This is essential if our culture is to survive.

In early 2020 the media played a couple of videos whereby radicalized conservative television and radio talk show hosts were talking about sacrificing senior citizens in an effort to revitalize the economy. Is this truly what the majority of Americans believe? Is this what we have become? Where is the humanity in such an idea?

Fortunately, these radicals do not represent the majority of Americans who believe in the human rights and civil liberties noted in this book. If Elijah Cummings, former civil rights leader and member of the United States House of Representatives for over twenty-two years, was still with us, he would most likely have said, "we are better than this." Most Americans are courageous citizens who, despite the fear of contracting the coronavirus and passing, go to work each day to help people in doctor's offices, hospitals, and emergency clinics. There are also firefighters, ambulance personnel and police who risk their life every day to help citizens in need. And, what about those Americans who work in grocery stores and warehouses, truckers, and so many others who work every day to deliver food and needed supplies to stores and consumers. They too expose themselves every day to this lethal virus in an effort to help others. These and more are the Americans who live in that shining city on the hill. These are the true Americans who help people all over the world in their time of need. This is the America most of us want to live in and want to see thrive in the future.

This book was written to serve as a reminder of how lucky we are to be living in America and who we are as Americans. It was also written to encourage a discussion on reforming and modernizing the United States federal government as soon as possible. If we are to keep our unique political, social and economic culture, Americans must not only practice those beliefs but do everything possible to make sure American culture endures.

Thank you again for reading this book. Now, get involved and help modernize our national government so the United States of America will last another three hundred years...

www.*ACallToReform*.com

Appendix

1789, *Declaration of the Rights of Man and of the Citizen*

As noted, the French Revolution began as a call to reform taxes by then French King Louis XVI. The treasury was almost bankrupt because of reckless spending and the assistance provided the Americans to break away from England and become independent. Remember, France not only provided an army to help general Washington and the Continental Army, but they also provided a fleet of ships. This fleet was instrumental in preventing British general Lord Cornwallis and his army from escaping at Yorktown. The French fleet under the command of Admiral DeGrass, successfully engaged the British fleet sent to embark Lord Cornwallis' army at Yorktown. At the Battle of the Virginia Capes, just outside the Chesapeake Bay on September 5, 1781, the French fleet was victorious. The British fleet was forced to withdraw and sail back to New York without evacuating Cornwallis and this army. The rest is history.

Unfortunately for King Louis XVI in France, things got out of hand rather quickly. Because of the help the French had given the Americans during the Revolutionary War, the treasury was near bankruptcy. Thus, King Louis XVI decided to call the Estates General into session. It had not met in over 200 years and was the only legal way the king could revise the tax structure.

However, when the delegates arrived in Paris from all provinces of France, it soon became clear they had come to enact reforms, in addition to discussing taxes. The delegates to the Estates General brought with them hundreds if not thousands of grievances they wanted addressed in the meeting of the Estates General. Louis XVI wanted none of that. He only wanted to revise the tax code to allow him to collect more taxes. So, he locked the delegates out of their meeting room. The French Revolution was on.

The purpose of this publication is not to go into any depth on the French Revolution. Readers are encouraged to study or read about the French Revolution on your own. It is fascinating but very violent and savage.

It is important to know, early on, the National Assembly (this body replaced the Estates General) promulgated a document, the *Declaration of the Rights of Man and of the Citizen*. Just like in *The Declaration of Independence*, the French document was to serve as a reminder why the revolution occurred in the first place and to remind future French governments that French Citizens are endowed with certain human rights and civil liberties. It was also to remind French Citizens to always maintain a constitution and promote the welfare of the people.

In this document we can see the influence of great philosophe writers. In addition, we can see the influence of American founding fathers and their embracement of many human rights and civil liberties in the founding of America. Many of these rights were eventually codified in both *The Constitution of the United States* and the *Bill of Rights* shortly before the French issued their document, *Declaration of the Rights of Man and of the Citizen*, in 1789. Below are the articles from the French document for your review:

1. Men are born free and remain free and equal in rights. Social distinctions can be based only on public utility.

2. The aim of every political association is the preservation of the natural and imprescriptible rights of man. These rights are liberty, property, security and resistance to oppression.

3. The sources of all sovereignty reside essentially in the nation; no body, no individual can exercise authority that does not proceed from it in plain terms.

4. Liberty consists in the power to do anything that does not injure others; accordingly, the exercise of the rights of each man has no limits except those that secure the enjoyment of these same rights to the other members of society. These limits can be determined only by law.

5. The law has only the rights to forbid such actions as are injurious to society. Nothing can be forbidden that is not interdicted by the law, and no one can be constrained to do that which it does not order.

6. Law is the expression of the general will. All citizens have the right to take part personally, or by their representatives, and its formation. It must be the same for all, whether it protects or punishes. All citizens, being equal in its eyes, are equally eligible to all public dignities, places, and employments, according to their capacities, and without other distinction than that of their virtues and talents.

7. No man can be accused, arrested, or detained, except in the cases determined by the law and according to the forms it has prescribed. Those who procure, expedite, execute, or cause arbitrary orders to be executed, ought to be punished: but every citizen summoned or seized in virtue of the law ought to render instant obedience; he makes himself guilty by resistance.

8. The law ought only to establish penalties that are strict and obviously necessary, and no one can be punished except in virtue of a law established and promulgated prior to the offense and legally applied.

9. Every man being presumed innocent until he has been pronounced guilty, if it is thought indispensable to

arrest him, all severity that may not be necessary to secure his person ought to be strictly suppressed by law.

10. No one should be disturbed on account of his opinions, even religious, provided their manifestation does not upset the public order established by law.

11. The free communication of ideas and opinions is one of the most precious of the rights of man; every citizen can then freely speak, write, and print, subject to responsibility for the abuse of this freedom in the cases determined by law.

12. The guarantee of the rights of man and citizen requires a public force; this force then is instituted for the advantage of all and not for the personal benefit of those to whom it is entrusted.

13. A general tax is indispensable for the maintenance of the public force and for the expenses of administration; it ought to be equally apportioned among all citizens according to their means.

14. All the citizens have a right to ascertain, by themselves or by their representatives, the necessity of the public tax, to consent to it freely, to follow the employment of it, and to determine the quota, the assessment, the collection, and the duration of it.

15. Society has the right to call for an account of his administration by every public agent.

16. Any society in which the guarantee of the rights is not secured, or the separation of powers not determined, has no constitution at all.

17. Property being a sacred to and inviolable right, no one can be deprived of it, unless legally established public necessity evidently demands it, under the condition of a just and prior indemnity (Anderson 58-60).

1948, United Nations Declaration of Human Rights

Below are the articles listing the *United Nations Declaration of Human Rights*. As you review them you will note many came from America. However, others are unique and represent the world's contribution to human rights and civil liberties. Some are still influencing American culture, even today.

Article

1. All human beings are born free and equal in dignity and rights. They are endowed with reason and conscience and should act towards one another in a spirit of brotherhood.

2. Everyone is entitled to all the rights and freedoms set forth in this Declaration, without distinction of any kind, such as race, color, sex, language, religion, political or other opinion, national or social origin, property, birth or other status. Furthermore, no distinction shall be made on the basis of the political, jurisdictional or international status of the country or territory to which a person belongs, whether it be independent, trust, non-self-governing or under any other limitation of sovereignty.

3. Everyone has the right to life, liberty and security of person.

4. No one shall be held in slavery or servitude; slavery and the slave trade shall be prohibited in all their forms.

5. No one shall be subjected to torture or to cruel, inhuman or degrading treatment or punishment.

6. Everyone has the right to recognition everywhere as a person before the law.

7. All are equal before the law and are entitled without any discrimination to equal protection of the law. All are entitled to equal protection against any discrimination in violation of this Declaration and against any incitement to such discrimination.

8. Everyone has the right to an effective remedy by the competent national tribunals for acts violating the fundamental rights granted him by the constitution or by law.

9. No one shall be subjected to arbitrary arrest, detention or exile.

10. Everyone is entitled in full equality to a fair and public hearing by an independent and impartial tribunal, in the determination of his rights and obligations and of any criminal charge against him.

11. (1) Everyone charged with a penal offence has the right to be presumed innocent until proved guilty according to law in a public trial at which he has had all the guarantees necessary for his defense.

    (2) No one shall be held guilty of any penal offence on account of any act or omission which did not constitute a penal offence, under national or international law, at the time when it was committed. Nor shall a heavier penalty be imposed than the one that was applicable at the time the penal offence was committed.

12. No one shall be subjected to arbitrary interference with his privacy, family, home or correspondence, nor to attacks upon his honor and reputation. Everyone has the right to the protection of the law against such interference or attacks.

13. (1) Everyone has the right to freedom of movement and residence within the borders of each state.

(2) Everyone has the right to leave any country, including his own, and to return to his country.

14. (1) Everyone has the right to seek and to enjoy in other countries asylum from persecution.

(2) This right may not be invoked in the case of prosecutions genuinely arising from non-political crimes or from acts contrary to the purposes and principles of the United Nations.

15. (1) Everyone has the right to a nationality.

(2) No one shall be arbitrarily deprived of his nationality nor denied the right to change his nationality.

16. (1) Men and women of full age, without any limitation due to race, nationality or religion, have the right to marry and to found a family. They are entitled to equal rights as to marriage, during marriage and at its dissolution.

(2) Marriage shall be entered into only with the free and full consent of the intending spouses.

(3) The family is the natural and fundamental group unit of society and is entitled to protection by society and the State.

17. (1) Everyone has the right to own property alone as well as in association with others.

(2) No one shall be arbitrarily deprived of his property.

18. Everyone has the right to freedom of thought, conscience and religion; this right includes freedom to change his religion or belief, and freedom, either alone or in community with others and in public or private, to manifest his religion or belief in teaching, practice, worship and observance.

19. Everyone has the right to freedom of opinion and expression; this right includes freedom to hold opinions without interference and to seek, receive and impart information and ideas through any media and regardless of frontiers.

20. (1) Everyone has the right to freedom of peaceful assembly and association.

(2) No one may be compelled to belong to an association.

21. (1) Everyone has the right to take part in the government of his country, directly or through freely chosen representatives.

(2) Everyone has the right of equal access to public service in his country.

(3) The will of the people shall be the basis of the authority of government; this will shall be expressed in periodic and genuine elections which shall be by universal and equal suffrage and shall be held by secret vote or by equivalent free voting procedures.

22. Everyone, as a member of society, has the right to social security and is entitled to realization, through national effort and international cooperation and in accordance with the organization and resources of each State, of the economic, social and cultural rights indispensable for his dignity and the free development of his personality.

23. (1) Everyone has the right to work, to free choice of employment, to just and favorable conditions of work and to protection against unemployment.

(2) Everyone, without any discrimination, has the right to equal pay for equal work.

(3) Everyone who works has the right to just and favorable remuneration ensuring for himself and his

family an existence worthy of human dignity, and supplemented, if necessary, by other means of social protection.

(4) Everyone has the right to form and to join trade unions for the protection of his interests.

24. Everyone has the right to rest and leisure, including reasonable limitation of working hours and periodic holidays with pay.

25. (1) Everyone has the right to a standard of living adequate for the health and well-being of himself and of his family, including food, clothing, housing and medical care and necessary social services, and the right to security in the event of unemployment, sickness, disability, widowhood, old age or other lack of livelihood in circumstances beyond his control.

(2) Motherhood and childhood are entitled to special care and assistance. All children, whether born in or out of wedlock, shall enjoy the same social protection.

26. (1) Everyone has the right to education. Education shall be free, at least in the elementary and fundamental stages. Elementary education shall be compulsory. Technical and professional education shall be made generally available and higher education shall be equally accessible to all on the basis of merit.

(2) Education shall be directed to the full development of the human personality and to the strengthening of respect for human rights and fundamental freedoms. It shall promote understanding, tolerance and friendship among all nations, racial or religious groups, and shall further the activities of the United Nations for the maintenance of peace.

(3) Parents have a prior right to choose the kind of education that shall be given to their children.

27. (1) Everyone has the right freely to participate in the cultural life of the community, to enjoy the arts and to share in scientific advancement and its benefits.

(2) Everyone has the right to the protection of the moral and material interests resulting from any scientific, literary or artistic production of which he is the author.

28. Everyone is entitled to a social and international order in which the rights and freedoms set forth in this Declaration can be fully realized.

29. (1) Everyone has duties to the community in which alone the free and full development of his personality is possible.

(2) In the exercise of his rights and freedoms, everyone shall be subject only to such limitations as are determined by law solely for the purpose of securing due recognition and respect for the rights and freedoms of others and of meeting the just requirements of morality, public order and the general welfare in a democratic society.

(3) These rights and freedoms may in no case be exercised contrary to the purposes and principles of the United Nations.

30. Nothing in this Declaration may be interpreted as implying for any State, group or person any right to engage in any activity or to perform any act aimed at the destruction of any of the rights and freedoms set forth herein, (The Universal Declaration of Human Rights).

List of Photographic Images and Illustrations

Adam Smith. (1085). Engraving. Library of Congress. Washington D.C.

Cesare Beccaria. FreeImages.com / Wpclipart.

Francois Marie Arouet de Voltaire. (1694-1778). Lithograph. Library of Congress. Washington D.C. Web.

Hader, E. Secondat du Montesquieu. (1880-1890). Photographic Print. Library of Congress. Washington D.C. Web.

Harriet Beecher Stowe. (1880). Photographic Print. Library of Congress. Washington D.C. Web.

Highsmith, Carol M. Rosie the Riveter mural on an abandoned building in Sacramento, California. (1946). Painting on a wall. Library of Congress. Washington D.C. Web.

Hollar, Wenceslaus. Cestina: Thomas Hobbes. (1665). Etching. National Gallery in Prague. Wikimedia Commons

John Locke. (1800-1899). Lithograph. Library of Congress. Washington D.C. Web.

John Maynard Keynes. FreeImages.com / Wpclipart.

Jean-Jacques Rousseau. Print. Library of Congress. Washington D.C. Web.

Leffler, Warren K. Coretta Scott King at the Democratic National Convention, New York City. (13 July 1976). Photograph. Library of Congress. Washington D.C. Web.

Lindsley, Harvey B. Harriet Tubman. (1871-1876). Photograph. Library of Congress. Washington D.C. Web.

McLaughlin, Andrew Cunningham. Proposed Divisions of Western Lands Ceded or To be Ceded according to Ordinance of April 23, 1783. (1905). | The American Nation: A History, Vol. 10 (27 vols.) The Confederation And the Constitution. (1783-1789). | Harper and Brothers Publishers, New York & London. (1905). 116+ Print. Also, from the Modern School Supply Company, and E.W.A. Rowles. The comprehensive series, historical-geographical maps of the United States. (Chicago, III: Modern School Supply Co, 1919) Map. Retrieved from the Library of Congress. www.loc.gov/item/2009581137/.

McLaughlin, Andrew Cunningham. State Claims to Western Lands 1783-1802. (1905). The American Nation: A History, Vol. 10 (27 vols.) The Confederation And the Constitution, 1783-1789). (1905). Harper and Brothers Publishers, New York & London. 108+ Print.

Rosa Parks. FreeImages.com / Wpclipart.

Sea Ice Extent. (2012). The National Snow and Ice Data Center (NSIDC) CIRES. Illustration. University of Colorado Boulder. Web.

Sojourner Truth. FreeImages.com / Wpclipart.

Stuart, Gilbert. Abigail Smith Adams wife of John Adams. Library of Congress. Photo of portrait by Gilbert Stuart. Washington D.C.

Works Cited

"18 U.S. Code Section 2340A. Torture." Legal Information Institute, 1992. Accessed 16 December 2019.

"18 U.S. Code Section 2441. War Crimes." Legal Information Institute, 1992. 16 December 2019.

"32 Powerful Quotes By Abigail Adams That Revealed Her Mind," www.thefamouspeople.com. Accessed 9 May 2019.

"Abigail Adams." History.com, updated: 6, March 2019, www.history.com. Accessed 9 May 2019.

"A Brief History of Human Rights…The Cyrus Cylinder 539 B.C." United for Human Rights, www.humanrights.com, Accessed 22 January 2019.

Abrams, Brigadier General Creighton W., USA-Ret., AHF Executive Director, "The Yorktown Campaign, October 1781." National Museum United States Army, 16 July 2014, www.armyhistory.org. Accessed 8 April 2019.

"Adolf Hitler Quotes," Brainy Quotes, 2001-2019, www.brainyquote.com. Accessed 27 January 2019.

"Ain't I A Woman?" Feminist.com, www.feminist.com. Accessed 9 May 2019.

Alperin, Elijah and Jeanne Batalova. "European Immigrants in the United States." Migration Policy Institute, 1 August 2018, www.migrationpolicy.org. Accessed 15 October 2019.

Alter, Charlotte. "Here's the History of the Battle for Equal Pay

for American Women." Time.com, 14, April 2015, www.time.
com. Accessed 9 May 2019.

Amadeo, Kimberly. "U.S. Military Budget, It's Components,
Challenges and Growth Why Military Spending is More Than
You Think It Is." TheBalance.com, Updated: 7, December
2019, www.thebalance.com. Accessed 13 June 2019.

Anderson, Frank Maloy. *Constitutions And Other Select*
Documents Illustrative Of The History of France 1789-1901.
Minneapolis The H.W. Wilson Company, 1904. Print. Library
of Congress: Digitized by Internet Archive, www.loc.gov.
Accessed 25 February 2020.

"Annual Update of the HHS Poverty Guidelines." Federal Register
The Daily Journal of the United States Government. A Notice
by the Health and Human Services Department, 18 January
2018. Accessed 2 January 2019.

"Articles of Confederation Transcript." Greatest Stories Ever Told,
2014, www.revolutionary-war.net. Accessed 4 January 2020.

"Asylum in the United States." American Immigration Council, 14
May 2018, www.americanimmigrationcouncil.org. Accessed
31 March 2019.

Barrington, Boyd C. Magna Carta and Other Great Charters of
England with an Historical Treaties and Copious Explanatory
Notes. Campbell Publishers. Philadelphia, 1900. Print.

Berger, Raoul. *Federalism The Founders' Design.* University of
Oklahoma Press: Norman and London: 1901/1987. Print.

Bernstein, Richard B. with Kym S Rice. *ARE WE TO BE A NATIION? The Making of the Constitution.* Harvard University Press: Cambridge, Massachusetts, And London, England, 1987. Print.

Brockman, Elin S. "American Jews Ellis Island A Brief History of the Place Where So Many Jewish Immigrants Entered the U.S." My Jewish Learning Center, www.myjewishlearning. com. Accessed 31 March 2019.

Bulger, Matthew. "The International Criminal Court: Why is the United States Not a Member?" The Humanist, 19 June 2013, thehumanist.com. Accessed 22 March 2019.

"Car Accident Statistics in the U.S." Driver Knowledge, www. driverknowledge.com. Accessed 22 December 2019.

"Children in Immigration Court: Over 95 Percent Represented by an Attorney in Court." American Immigration Council, 16 May 2016, www.americanimmigrationcouncil.org. Accessed 25 March 2019.

"Cesare Beccaria." Famous Philosophers, 2019. Accessed 8 August 2019. www.famousphilosophers.org/cesare-beccaria/.

Cohn, Marjorie. "Under U.S. Law Torture is Always Illegal." Counter Punch, 6 May 2008, www.counterpunch.org. Accessed 15 February 2019.

Colden, Cadwalladord. *The History of the Five Indian Nations of Canada. Vol. 2.* New York, Amsterdam Book Co. Publishers, 1902. Print.

Condon, Stephanie, "Poll: One in Four Americans Think Obama Was Not Born in the U.S.." CBS News/April 21, 2011/8:05 pm. CBS News, 21 April 2011. Accessed 12 April 2019.

"Congress renames the nation *United States of America*." History.com, 1 September 2010, Updated: 5 September 2019, www.history.com. Accessed 11 April 2019.

"Convention Against Torture and Other Cruel, Inhuman Or Degrading Treatment or Punishment." Audiovisual Library of International Law. Legal.un.org, 10 December 1984, www.legal.un.org. Accessed 25 September 2019.

Crosby, Alfred W., Jr., "The Columbian Exchange." Westport, Connecticut, GREENWOOD PRESS, INC, 1972. Print.

"Current Spending." UK Public Spending Co. UK., www.ukpublicspendingco.uk. Accessed 23 December 2019.

Das, Andrew. "U.S. Women's Soccer Team Sues Soccer for Gender Discrimination." New York Times, 8 March 2019, www.nytimes.com/2019/03/08/sports/womens-soccer-team-lawsuit-gender-discrimination.html. Accessed 25 July 2019.

Data Analysis & Documentation Federal Employment Reports. U.S. Office of Personnel Manage ment. Accessed 17 February 2019.

"Declaration of Independence: A Transcription." National Archives, 19 November 2019, www.archives.gov. Accessed 6 October 2019.

"Definitive Treaty of Peace Between The United States And Great

Britain, 3 September 1783." National Archives Founders online. Accessed 19 November 2019.

"Denis Diderot." HumanistsUK.com, humanism.org.uk. Accessed 6 November 2019.

Duffin, Erin. "Number of People Living Below the Poverty Line in the United States from 1990 to 2018." Statista. 18 September 2019, www.statista.com. Accessed 3 October 2019.

Duganan, Brian. "What is the Emoluments Clause." Encyclopedia Britannica, www.britannica.com. Accessed 18 October 2019.

Erb, Kelly Phillips, "For Election Day, A History of the Poll Tax in America." Forbes, 5 November 2018, www.forbes.com. Accessed 27 February 2019.

"Facts Income Inequality in the United States Gaps in the Earnings Between America's Most Affluent and the Rest of Country Continue to Grow Year After Year." Inequality.org, www.inequality.org. Accessed 28 February 2019.

"Fifty Famous Quotes by Hitler." Quotesigma.com, www.quotesigma.com. Accessed 27 January 2019.

"Firearm Suicide in the United States." Everytown for Gun Safety, 30 August 2019, www.everytownresearch.org. Accessed 21 December 2019.

"George Wilhelm Friedrich Hegel." PhilosophyBasics.com, www.philosophybasics.com. Accessed 16 December 2019.

Glenza, Jessica. "Abuse of Teen Inmate at Rikers Island Prison Caught on Surveillance Cameras." The Guardian, 24 April

2015, www.theguardian.com. Accessed 5 January 2019.

Glum, Julia, "Some Republicans Still Think Obama was Born
in Kenya as Trump Resurrects Birther Conspiracy Theory."
Newsweek, 11 December 2017, www.newsweek.com.
Accessed 12 April 2019.

Gonnerman, Jennifer. "KALIEF BROWDER 1993-2015." The
New Yorker, 7 June 2015, www.newyorker.com. Accessed 5
February 2019.

Gardner, Amy, "In North Carolina A Surprise: In the End,
Everyone Agreed it Was Election Fraud." The Washington
Post in The Chicago Tribune, 23 February 2019, www.
washingtonpost.com. Accessed 27 February 2019.

"George Washington September 17, 1796 Farewell Address." The
Library of Congress, www.loc.gov. Accessed February 2019.

"Germany-Military Spending." GlobalSecurity.org, www.
globalsecurity.org. Accessed 23 December 2019.

"Gotthold Ephraim Lessing." New World Encyclopedia, www.
newworldencyclopedia.org. Accessed 15 December 2019.

Graebner, Norman A., Gilbert C. Fite, Philip L. White. *A History
of the American People*. New York: McGraw Hill Book
Company, 1970. Print.

Griffin, Jeff. "The History of Healthcare in America." J.P. Griffin
Group, 7 March 2017, www.griffinbenefits.com. Accessed 20
April 2019.

"H.R.1 - For the People Act of 2019," Congress.Gov. Passed

House: 8 March 2019, www.congress.gov. Accessed 10 May 2019.

Hellmann, Melissa. "U.S. Healthcare Ranks Worst in the Developed World." Time. 17 June 2014, www.time.com. Accessed 4 March 2019.

Henny, Megan. "Amazon earned $6.5 billion in 2017 but paid no federal taxes." Fox Business News, 2017, www.foxbusiness. com. Accessed 11 July 2019.

"Here's how much a US missile attack in Syria costs." Daily Sabah, 4 July 2017, Updated: 4 November 2018, www.dailysabah. com. Accessed 11 July 2019.

Hibbard, Devin, M.P.A., Gilda Wheeler, M.Ed., and Wendy Church, Ph.D. "Global Issues & SUSTAINABLE SOLUTONS Population, Poverty, Consumption, Conflict And The Environment. Seattle: Facing the Future: People and the Planet." 2004. Print.

History.com Editors. "Electoral College," History.com, 12 January 2010, Updated: 27 September 2019, www.history.com. Accessed 19 March 2019.

History.com Editors. "Geneva Convention." History.com, 17 November 2017, Updated: 21 August 2018, www.history.com. Accessed 10 September 2019.

History.com Editors. "Judicial Branch," History.com, 17 November 2017, Updated: 21 August 2018, www.history.com. Accessed 12 April 2019.

History.com Editors. "Harriet Tubman." History.com, 29 October 2009, Updated: 15 April 2019, www.history.com. Accessed 9 May 2019.

History.com Editors. "Jim Crow Laws." History.com, 28 February 2018, Updated: 19 December 2019, www.history.com. Accessed 20 February 2019.

History.com Editors. "The KKK kills three civil rights activists." History.com, 13 November 2009, Updated: 27 July 2019, www.history.com. Accessed 7 August 2019.

History.com Editors. "Medgar Evers." History.com, 9 November 2019, Updated: 21 March 2019, www.history.com. Accessed 25 July 2019.

History.com Editors. "Rosie the Riveter." History.com, 23 April 2010, Updated: 13 September 2019, www.history.com. Accessed 25 October 2019.

History.com Editors. "Seneca Falls Convention." History.com, 10 November 2017, Updated: 20 November 2019, www.history.com. Accessed 9 May 2019.

History.com Editors. "Shays Rebellion." History.com, 12 November 2009, updated 31 October 2019, www.history.com. Accessed 5 January 2019.

History.com Editors. "Sojourner Truth." History.com, Updated: 2 November 2018, www.history.com. Accessed 9 May 2019.

History.com Editors. "Susan B. Anthony." History.com, Updated: August 21, 2018, www.history.com. Accessed 9 May 2019.

History.com Editors. "Transcontinental Railroad." History.com, 20 April 2010, Updated: 11 September 2019, www.history. com. Accessed 30 March 2019.

History.com Editors. "U.S. Constitution Ratified." History.com, 24 Nov. 2009, Updated: 28 July 2019, www.history.com. Accessed 5 September 2019.

Hobbes, Thomas (Edited by C.B. Macpherson). *Leviathan*, 1651. London: Penguin Books, 1868. Print.

"Household Data Annual Averages 1. Employment Status of the Civilian noninstitutional population, 1948 to date (Number in thousands)." United States Department of Labor, Bureau of Labor Statistics, Labor Force Statistics from the Current Population Survey, www.bls.gov. Accessed October 25, 2019.

"Household Data Annual Averages 35. Persons not in the labor force by desire and availability for work, age, and sex (Number in thousands)." United States Department of Labor, Bureau of Labor Statistics, Labor Force Statistics from the Current Population Survey, www.bls.gov. Accessed October 25, 2019.

Howard, Jacqueline, CNN, "Gun deaths in US reach highest level in nearly 40 years, CDC data reveal." CNN, 14 December 2018, www.cnn.com. Accessed 26 April 2019.

"Journals of Congress, Paper No. VIII." Library of Congress American Memory A Century of Lawmaking for a New Nation: U.S. Congressional Documents and Debates, 1774-

1875. Journals of the Continental Congress, volume 24, www. loc.gov. 14 January 2020.

"King Charles I of England." Totally History, 2012. Accessed 2 August 2019.

Landrum, Ryan. "Where did the phrase 'all men are created equal' come from?" Quora, 25 July 2015, www.quora.com. Accessed February 2019.

Le, C.N. "The First Asian Americans." Asian Nation Asian American History, Demographics, & Issues, 2001-2019, www. asian-nation.org. Accessed March 2019.

Lee, Richard Henry. *Journals of the Continental Congress*, volume 5, in the writing of Richard Henry Lee, Papers of the Continental Congress, No. 23, folio 11, 7 June 1776, www. memory.loc.gov. Accessed 18 January 2020.

Lewis, Jone Johnson. "Abigail Adams Quotes." ThoughtCo.com, 13 April 2019, www.thoughtco.com. Accessed 10 July 2019.

Liberto, Jennifer. "Millionaire ask Congress to raise their Taxes." CNN Money.com, November 16, 2011, www. money.cnn. com. Accessed 2 March 2019.

"Like a house on fire: Washington to Henry Knox," February 3, 1787.

Locke, John. *Two Treatises of Government*, 1698. New Jersey: The Classics of Liberty Library. 1992. Print.

"London's Original and All-Inspiring Coffee House." Atlas Obscura, www.atlasobscura.com. Accessed 15 December

2019.

Longley, Robert. "What Was Jay's Treaty." ThoughtCo.com, 12
October 2018, www.thoughtco.com. Accessed 28 August
2019.

Manz, Bruno. *A Mind In Prison: The Memoir of a Son and Soldier
of the Third Reich*. Washington D.C.. Brassey's, 2000. Print.

McKechnie, William Sharp. *Magna Carta A Commentary on The
Great Charter of King John With an Historical Introduction
by William Sharp McKechnie, M.A., L.L.B., D.Phil*. Glasgow:
James Maclehose and Sons Publishers to the University, 1905.
Print.

McLaughlin, Andrew Cunningham, Director of the Bureau of
Historical Research Carnegie Institution. *The American
Nation: A History, Vol. 10 (27 vols.) The Confederation And
the Constitution, 1783-1789*. Harper and Brothers Publishers,
New York & London, 1905. Print.

Medieval Sourcebook: Magna Carta 1215. Fordham University,
sourcebooks.fordham.edu. Accessed 17 January 2019.

"Nepotism." Merriam-Webster, merriam-webster.com. Accessed
10 November 2018.

Mil, Duncan. "China's military goes from strength to strength
under Xi Jinping." Graphic News, 3 April 2019, www.
graphicnews.com. Accessed 5 April 2019.

"Military Spending By Country 2019." World Population Review,
24 October 2019, worldpopulationreview.com. Accessed 30

November 2019.

"Executive Orders 101: What are they and How do Presidents Use Them." National Constitution Center, 23 January 2017, constitutioncenter.org. Accessed 12 October 2019.

"Newburgh Conspiracy." *George Washington's Mount Vernon*, www.mountvernon.org. Accessed November 19, 2019.

"Our Government The Judicial Branch." Whitehouse.gov, www. whitehouse.gov. Accessed 15 September 2019.

O'Sullivan, Arthur & Sheffrin, Steven. *Economics: Principles In Action*. Boston, Massachusetts; Upper Saddle River, New Jersey: Pearson Prentice Hall. 2007. Print.

Payne, Samuel B. Jr. "The Iroquois League, the Articles of Confederation, and the Constitution." *The William and Mary Quarterly Vol. 53, No. 3*, July 1996, www.jstor.org. Accessed 15 September 2019.

Plen, Matt. "Mendelssohn Herald of the Jewish Enlightenment." My Jewish Learning, www.myjewishlearning.com. Accessed 5 November 2019.

Ridpath, John Clark, LL.D. *History of the United States Epochs of Discovery, Planting and Independence*. Washington D.C., The American Historical Society, by E.J. Stanley, 1900. Print.

Roland, John. "The Petition of Right 1628." Constitution Society, 18 October 1998, updated 5 December 2019, www. constitution.org. Accessed 23 January 2019.

Roos, Dave. "Was George Washington Really Offered a Chance

to be King of the United States." History.HowStuffWorks. com, 31 July 2018, history.howstuffworks.com. Accessed 19 November 2019.

Rosling, Hans. "Don't Panic, the Truth About Population." YouTube, 7 November 2013, www.youtube.com. Accessed 15 May 2019.

Rousseau, Jean-Jacques, Du Contract Social bk. 1, ch. 1, (1762). AZQuotes.com, www.azquotes.com. Accessed 24 July 2019.

Rubenstein, Grace. "New Health Rankings: Of 17 Nations, U.S. is dead last." The Atlantic, 10 January 2013, www.theatlantic. com. Accessed 4 March 2019.

Salles, Joaquim Moreira. "The Wealth Gap Between Rich And Poor Is The Widest Ever Recorded." ThinkProgress.org, 18 December 2014, archive.thinkprogress.org. Accessed 28 February 2019.

Sawyer, Bradley and Cox, Cynthia. "How does health spending in the U.S. compare to other countries?" Kaiser Family Foundation, Peterson-KFF Health System Tracker, December 7, 2018, www.healthsystemtracker.org. Accessed 22 April 2019.

"Sep 22, 1862 Abraham Lincoln Issues First Order of Emancipation Proclamation." WorldHistoryProject.org, 20 October 2018, worldhistoryproject.org. Accessed 11 March 2019.

Shah, Anup. "Poverty Facts and Stats." Global Issues Social,

Political, Economic and Environmental Issues That Affect Us All Updated 7 January 2013, www.globalissues.org. Accessed 29 December 2019.

Smith, Goldwin. *Three English Statemen: A Course of Lectures on the Political History of England*. New York: Harper and Brothers Publishers Franklin Square, 1879. Print.

"Sojourner Truth." SojournerTruth.com, www.sojournertruth. com. Accessed 9 May 2019.

Stewart, David O. *The Summer of 1787: The Men Who Invented the Constitution*. New York: Simon and Schuster, 2007. Print.

Student Bible New International Version; Notes by Philip Yancey and Tim Stafford. Grand Rapids, Michigan. Zondervan, 1973, 1978, 1984. Print.

"SUPREME COURT OF THE UNITED STATES Syllabus TIMBS v. INDIANA." Supremecourt.org, 18 October 2018, www. supremecourt.gov. Accessed 15 September 2019.

"The Bill of Rights: A Transcription." National Archives, America's Founding Documents, www.archives.gov. Accessed 10 October 2019.

"Transcription of Articles of Confederation." National Archives, www.archives.gov. Accessed 11 April 2019.

"The Civil War, Charles I and the Petition of Right." parliament. uk, www.parliament.uk. Accessed 23 January 2019.

"The Constitutional Convention." ConstitutionFacts.com, www. constitutionfacts.com. Accessed 17 February 2019.

"The Coffee Houses of London," www.Blackapollo.demon.co.uk. Accessed 15 December 2019.

"The Constitution of the United States: A Transcription." National Archives America's Founding Documents, www.archives.gov. Accessed 12 March 2019.

"The Delegates Who Didn't Sign the U.S. Constitution." ConstitutionFacts.com, www.constitutionfacts.com. Accessed 7 February 2019.

"The Distribution of Household Income 2016." Congressional Budget Office, 2016, www.cbo.gov. Accessed 9 July 2019.

"The Freedom of Assembly Clause." Revolutionary War and Beyond, www.revolutionary-war-and-beyond.com. Accessed 10 January 2019.

"The Impact of Executive Branch Secrecy on the United States' Compliance with the Convention Against Torture and other Cruel Inhumane or Degrading Treatment or Punishment." *Shadow Report Prepared for the 53rd Session of the United Nations Committee Against Torture in Connection with its Review of the United States.* Open the Government, 2014, www.openthegovernment.org. Accessed 10 February 2019.

"The Reichstag Burns." The History Place The Rise of Adolf Hitler. Historyplace.com, 1996, www.historyplace.com. Accessed November 3, 2019.

"The Universal Declaration of Human Rights." United Nations, www.un.org. Accessed 21 January 2019 & 28 March 2019.

"The Vikings in Newfoundland." Historica Canada, 1 February 2010, www.historicacanada.ca. Accessed 30 March 2019.

"The World Factbook." Central Intelligence Agency, www.cia.gov. Accessed 7 March 2019.

"Top 25 Destinations of International Migrants." Migration Policy Institute, 2017, www.migrationpolicy.org. Accessed 31 March 2019.

"Timeline for Women's Rights." Digital History, www.digitalhistory.uh.edu. Accessed 24 July 2019.

"To Henry Knox, Mount Vernon, February 3, 1787." *George Washington Papers, Series 2, Letterbooks 1754-1799*. Library of Congress, www.loc.gov. Accessed 18 December 2019.

"What Are Cesare Beccaria's Beliefs." Reference.com, www.reference.com. Accessed 15 December 2019.

"What is the Divine Right Theory of Government," www.reference.com. Accessed 10 June 2019.

"White Only: Jim Crow in America. Separate is not Equal Brown vs. Board of Education." Smithsonian National Museum of American History, americanhistory.si.edu. Accessed 20 July 2019.

"Who Were the Roundheads?" WiseGEEK clear answers for common questions, www.wisegeek.com. Accessed October 31, 2019.

Wolf, Richard. "Supreme Court Strikes blow against states that raise revenue by hefty fines, forfeitures." USA Today, 20

February 2019, www.usatoday.com. Accessed 5 March 2019.

Zhao, Xiaojian, "Immigration to the United States after 1945." American History online, July 2016, oxfordre.com. Accessed 10 October 2019.

www.*ACallToReform*.com

Made in the USA
Middletown, DE
25 August 2020